Roller Skate Girls

Deanna Harrison

ISBN:1540758060
ISBN-13:9781540758064

Cover Colorist

Loraine Wilson

This Book Belongs To

_____

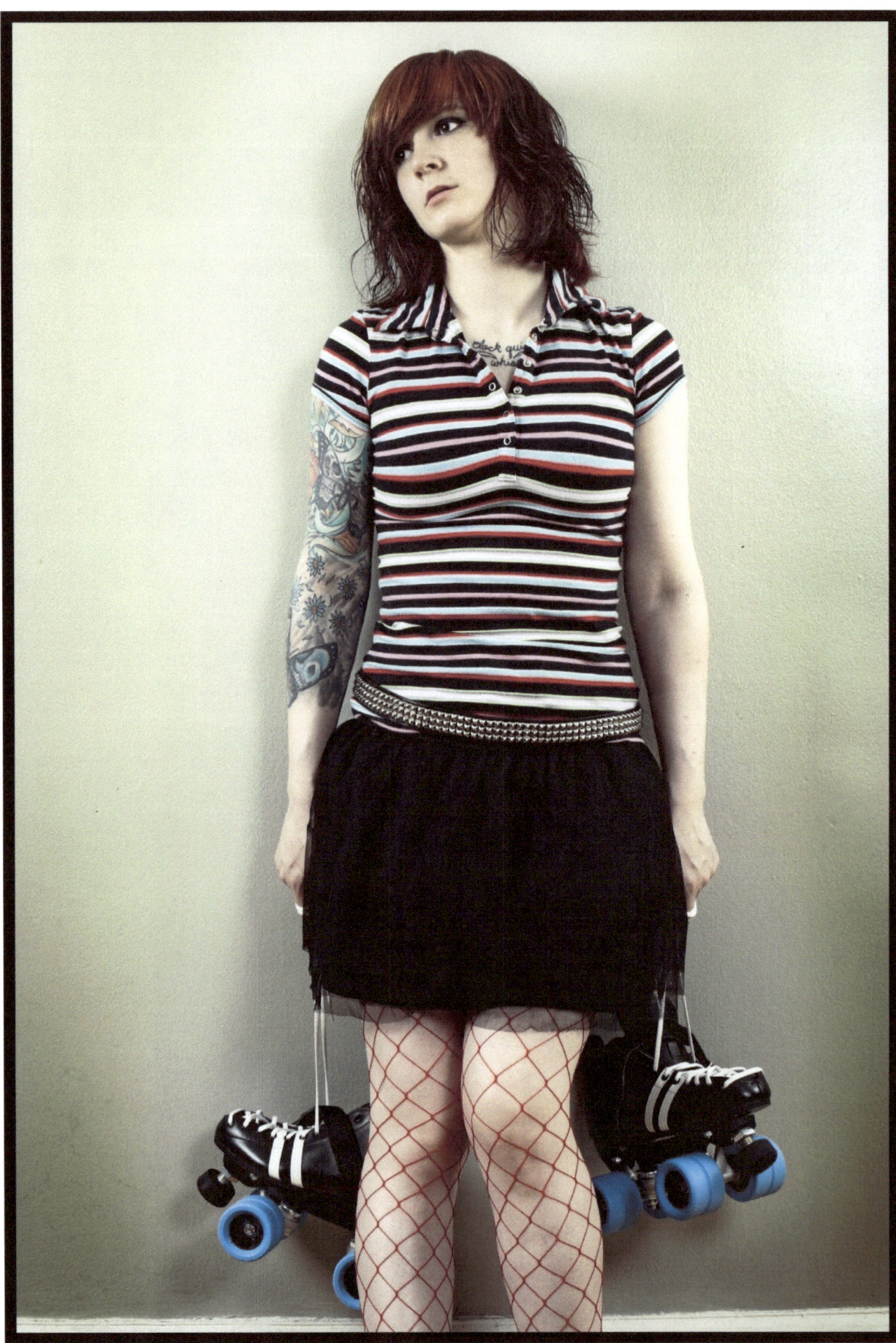

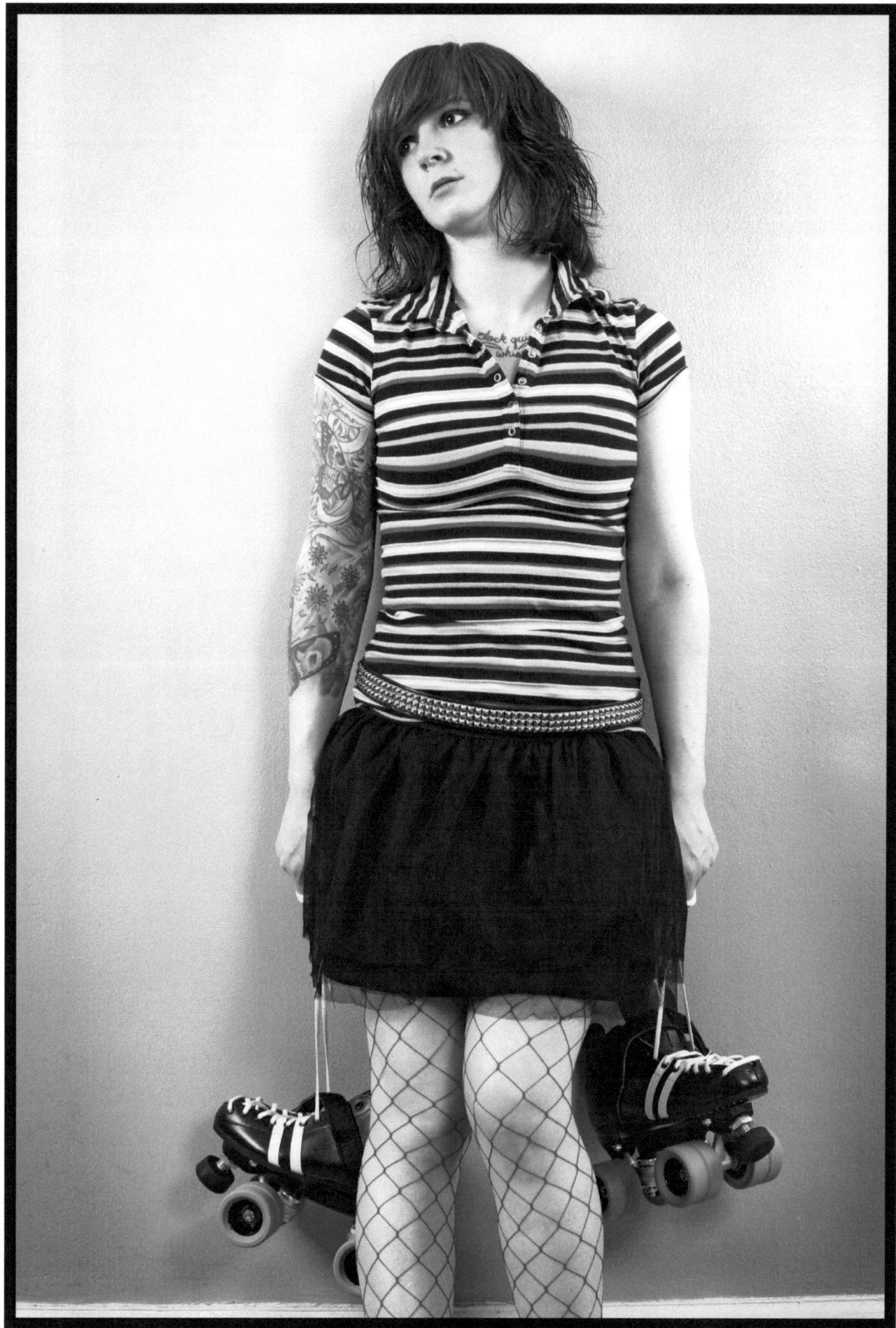

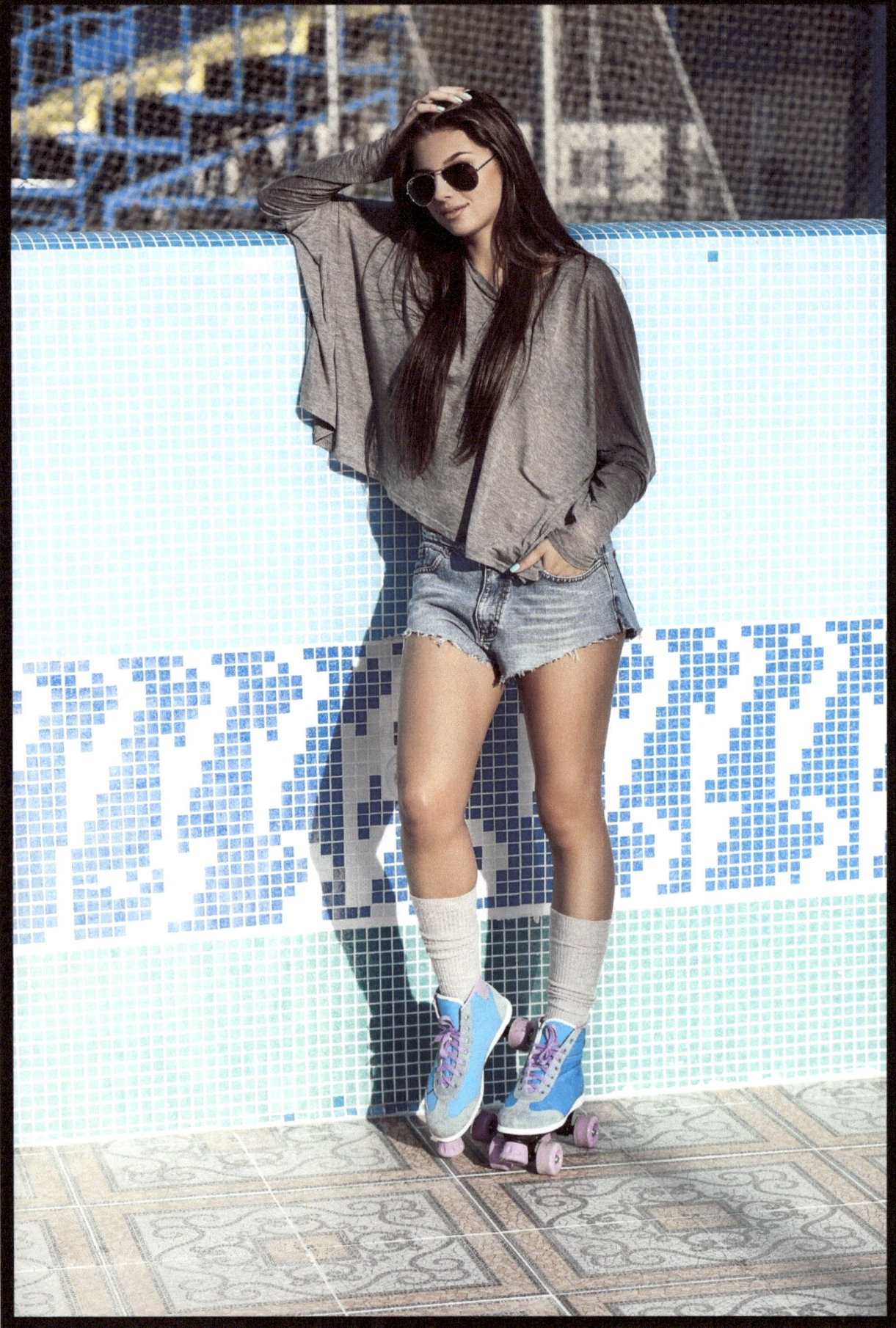

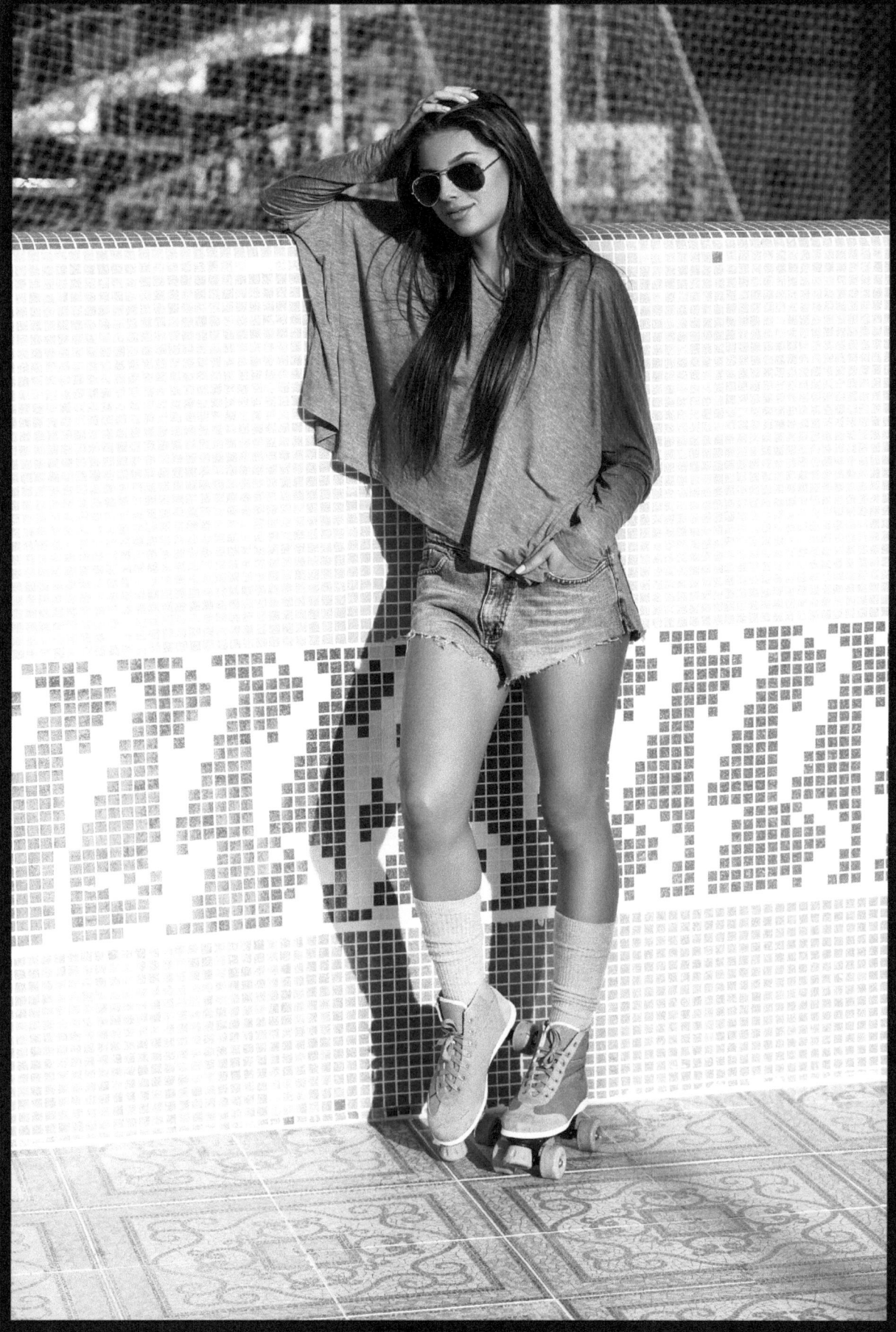

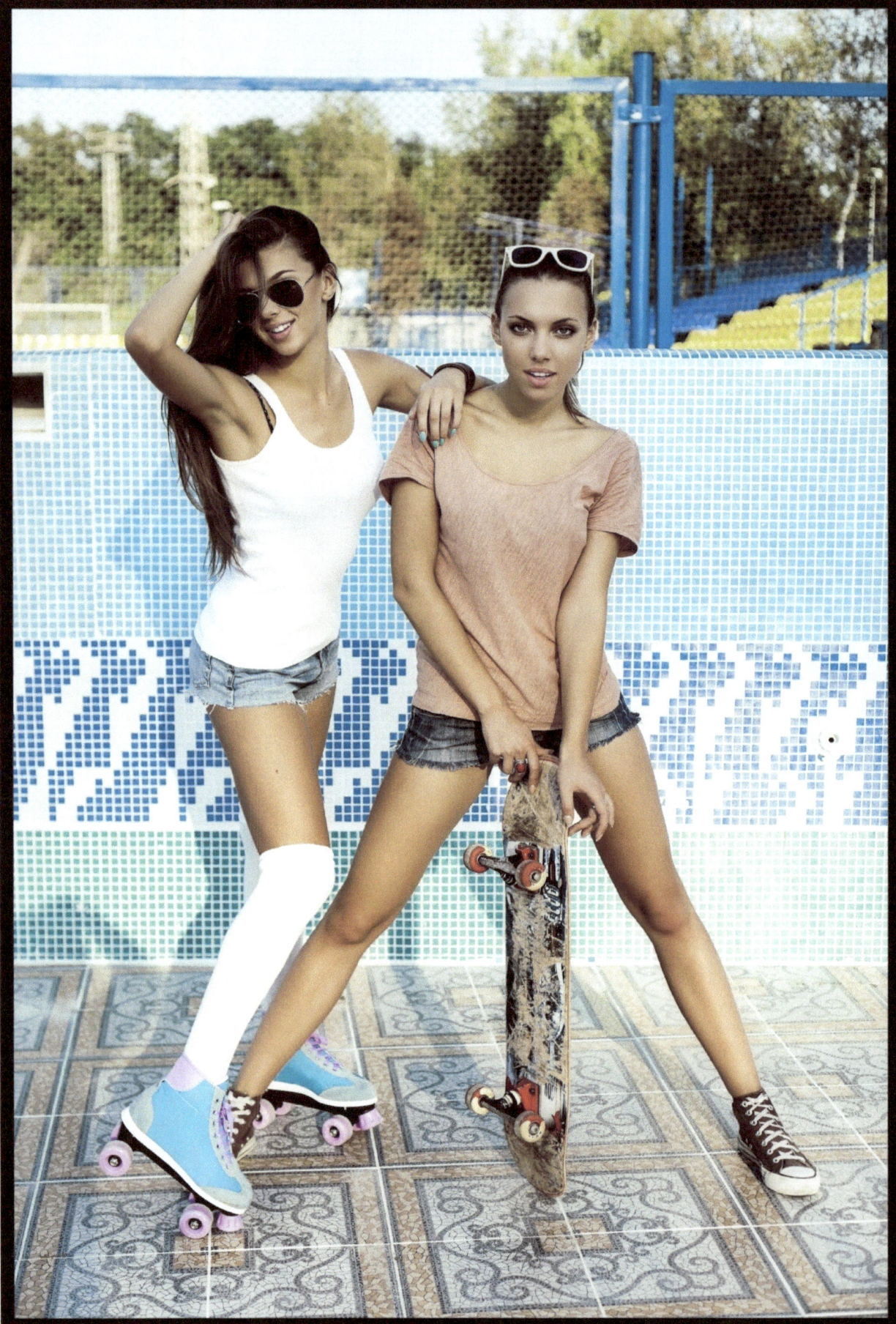

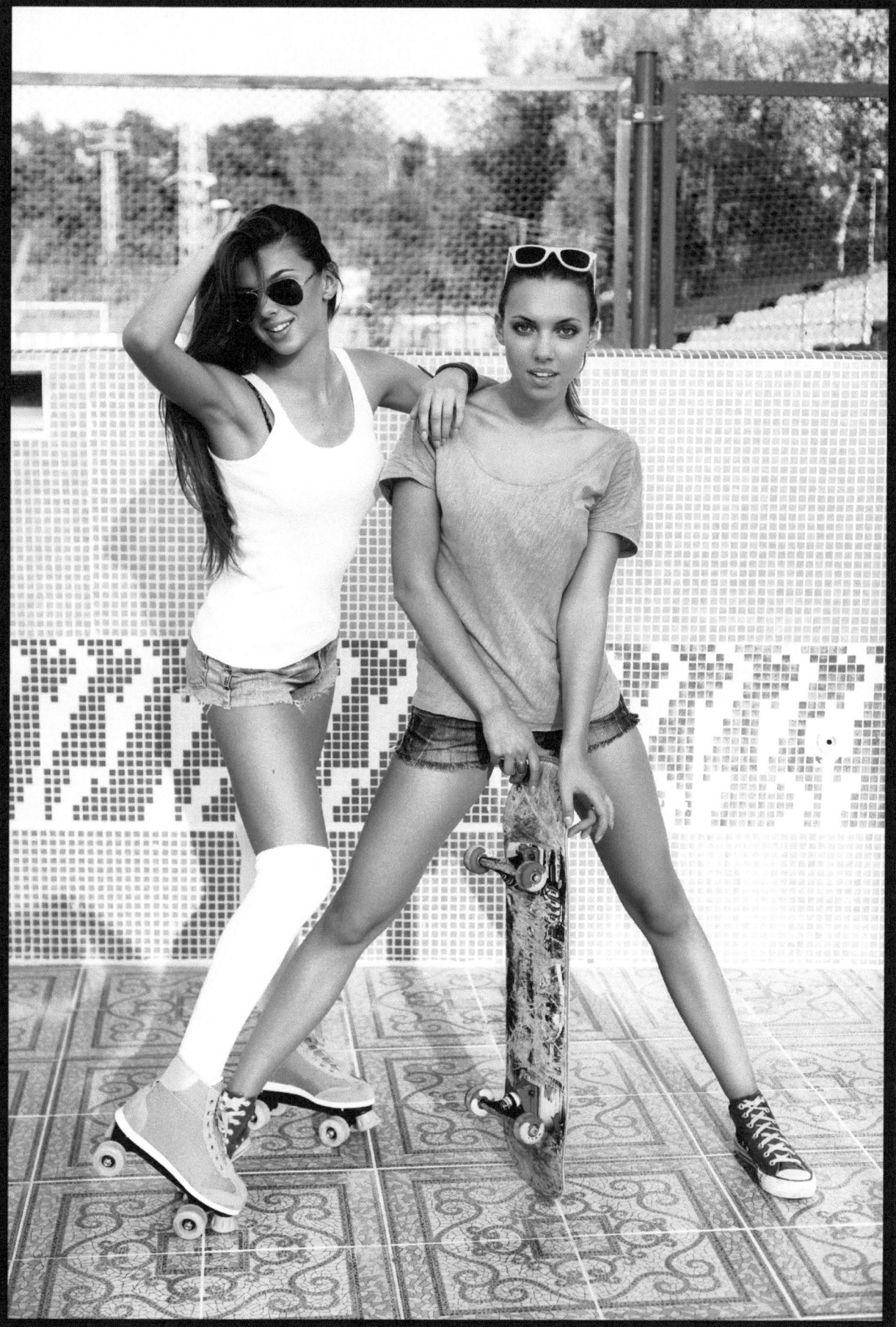

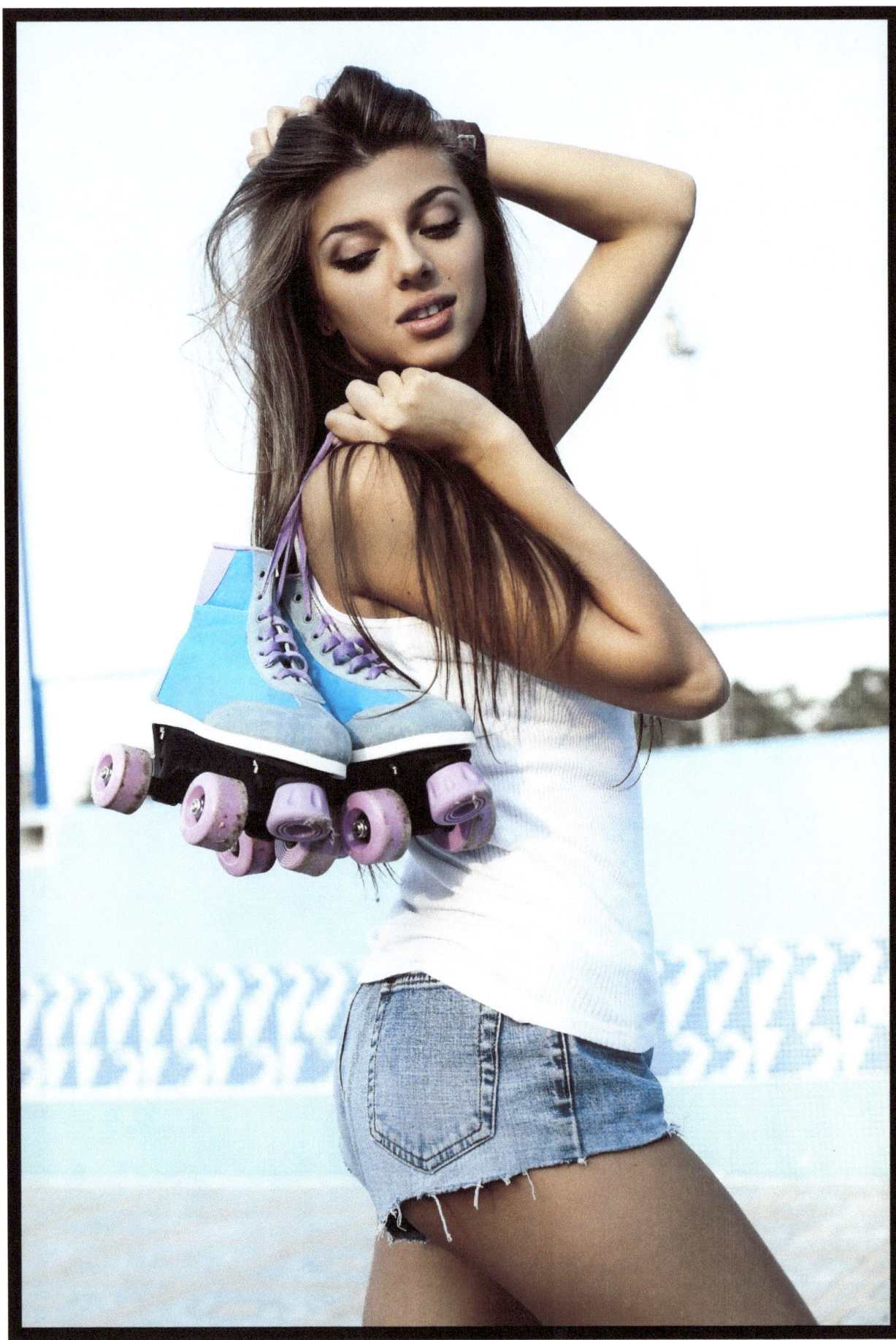

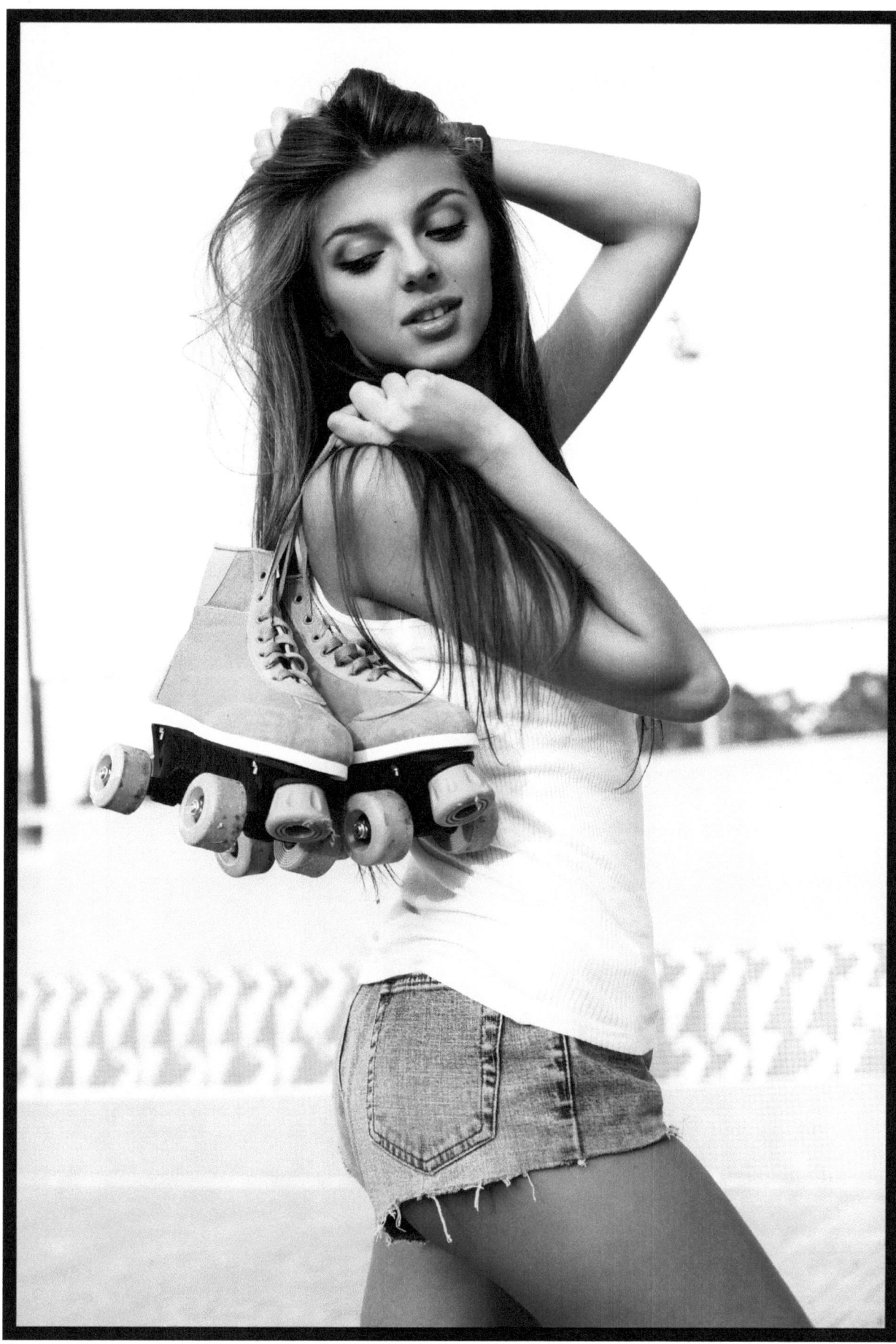

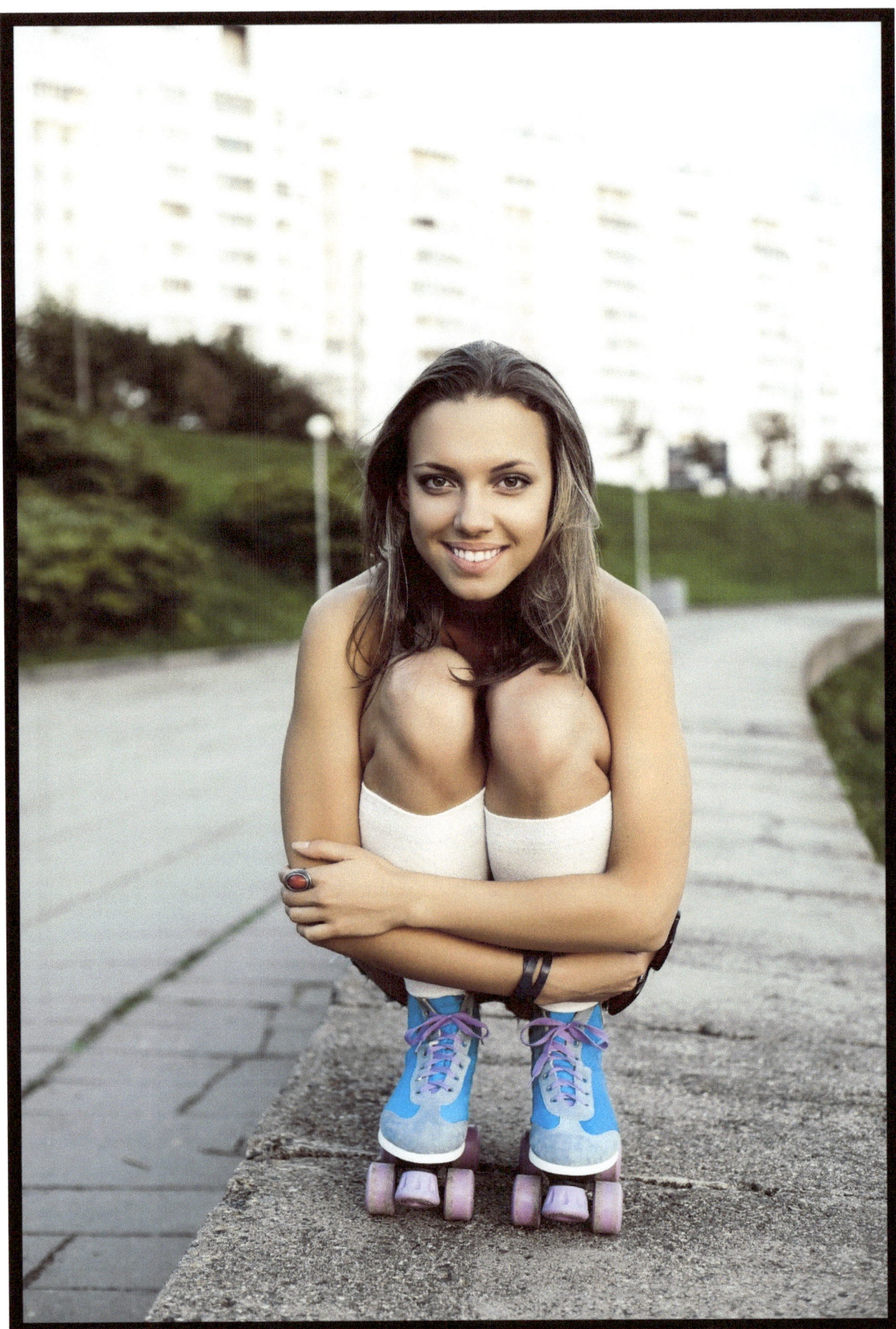

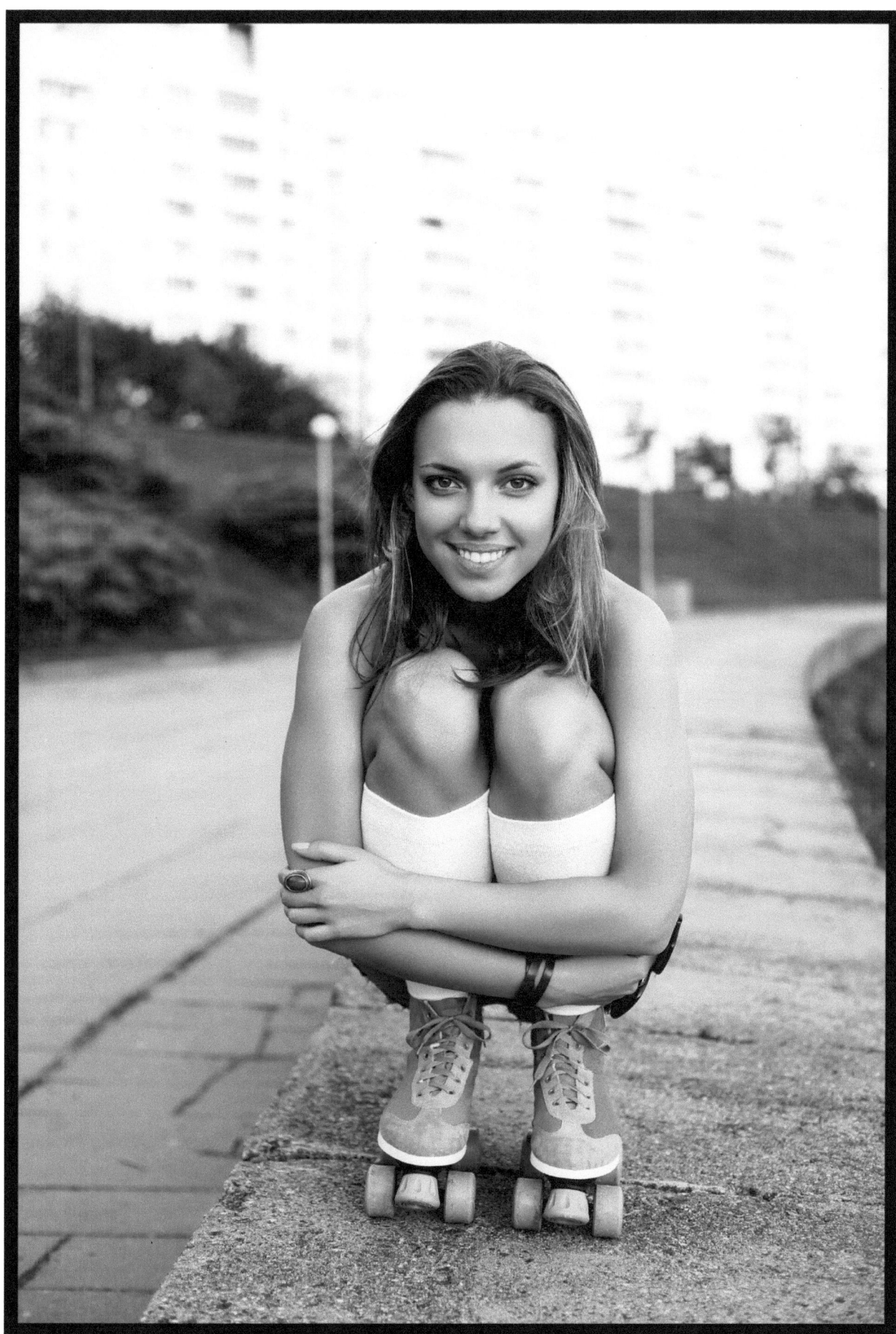

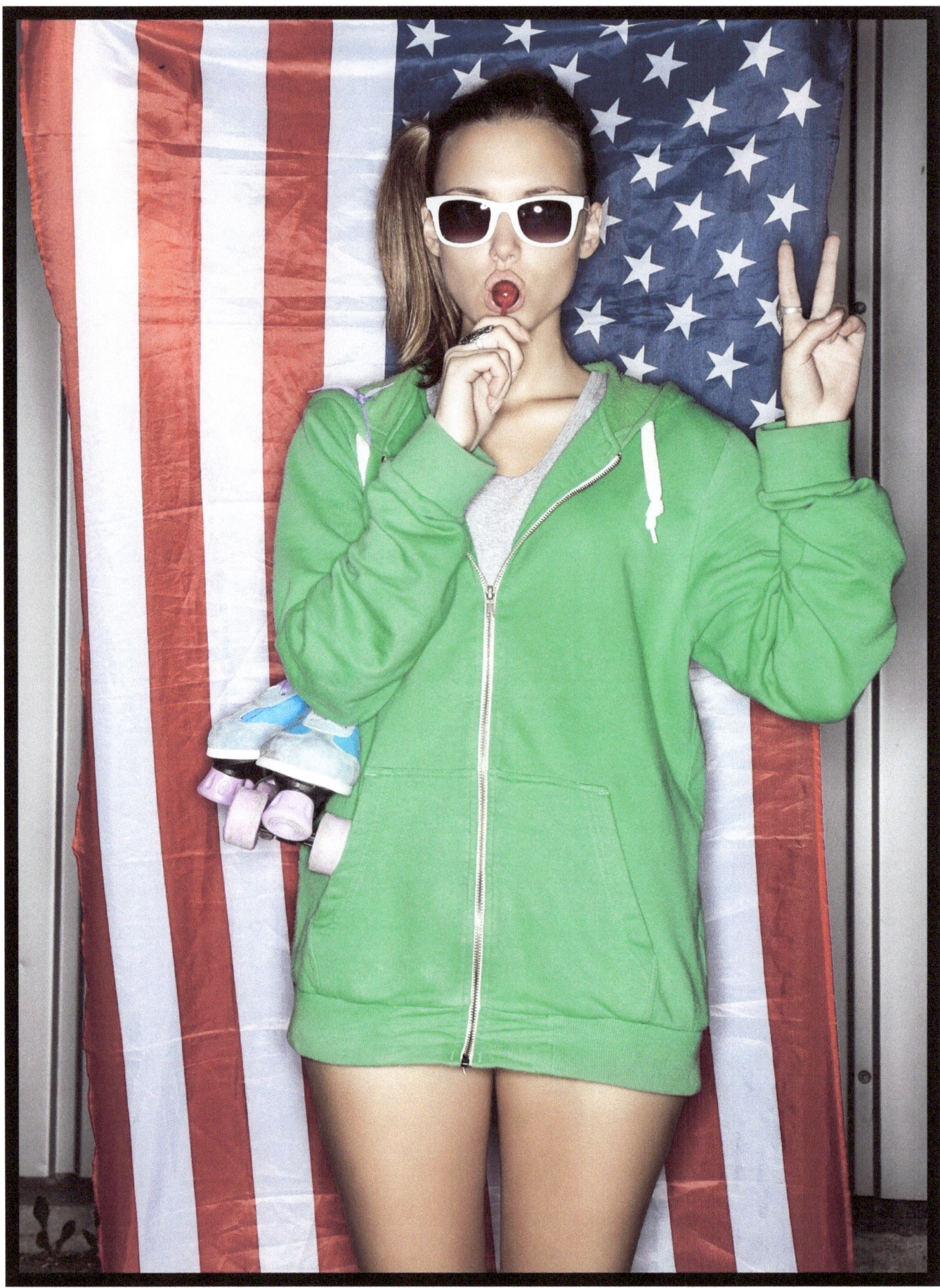

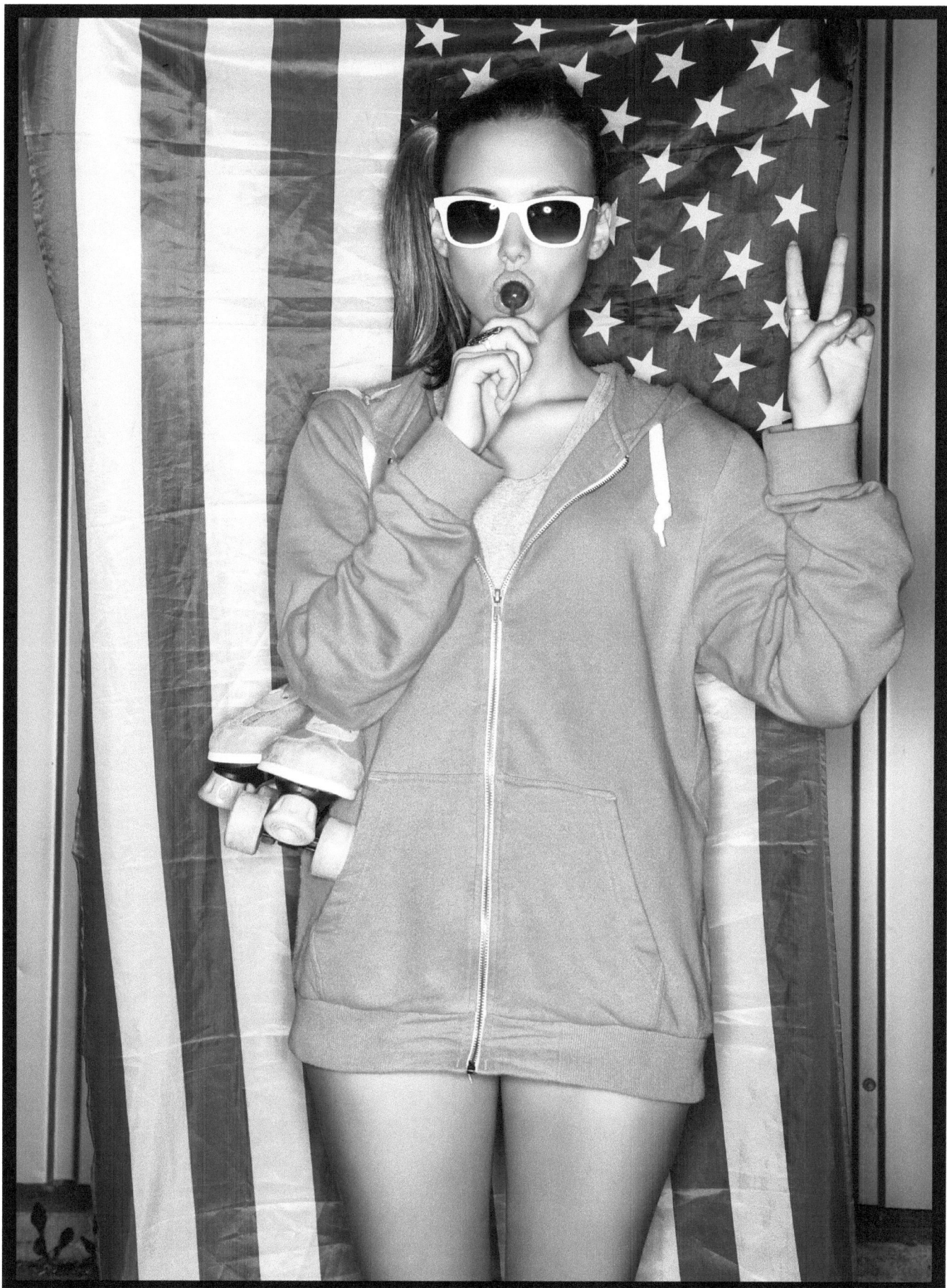

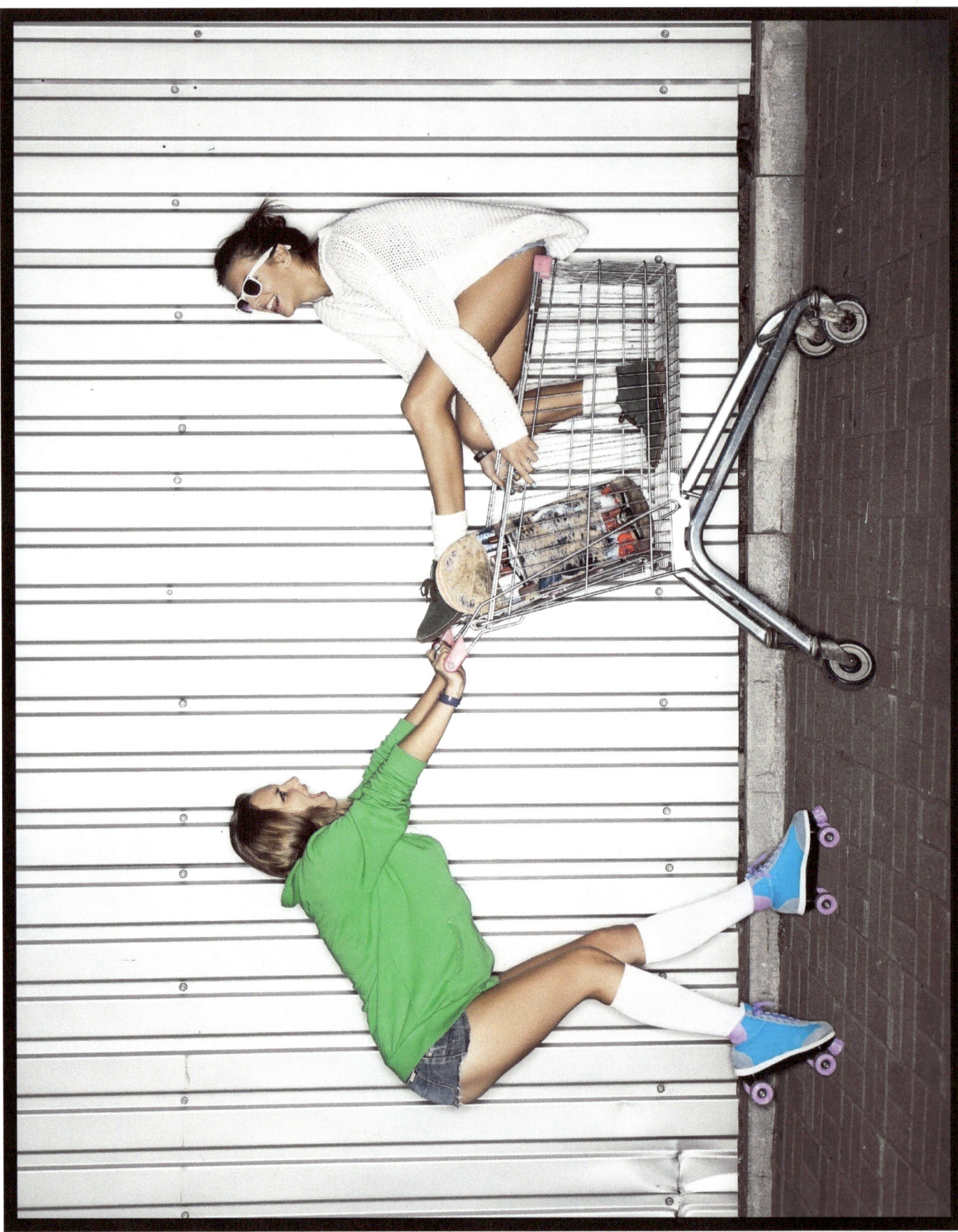

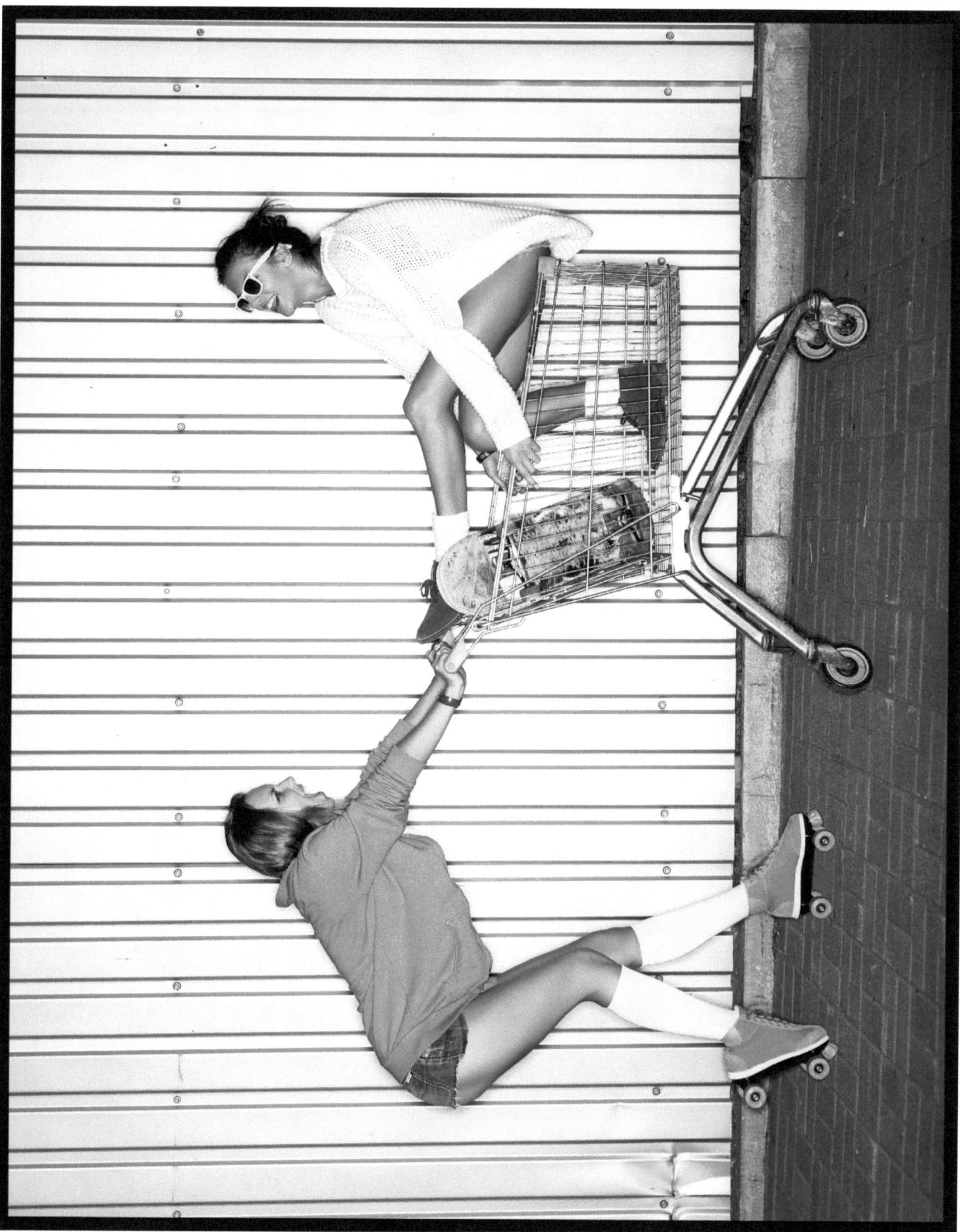

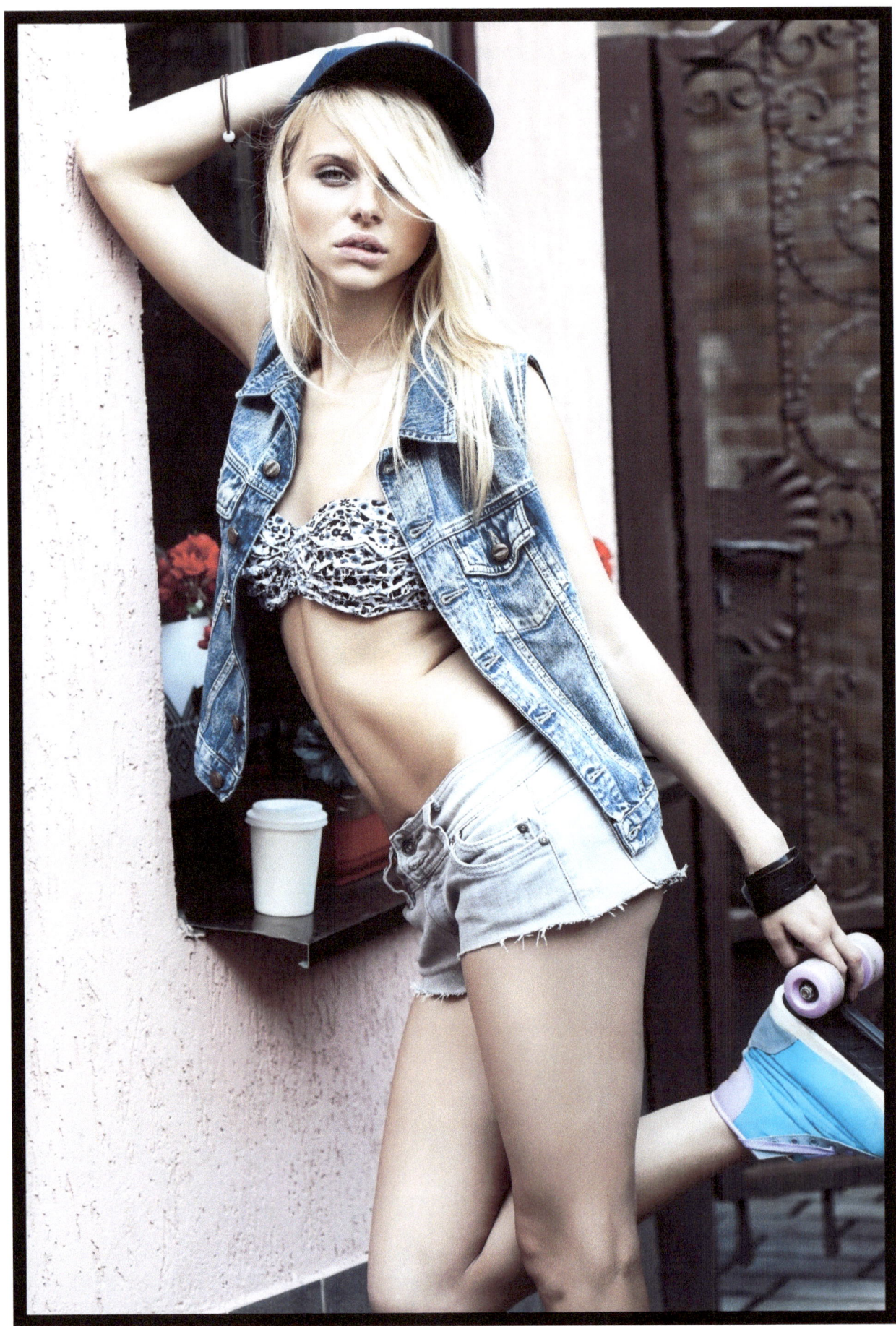

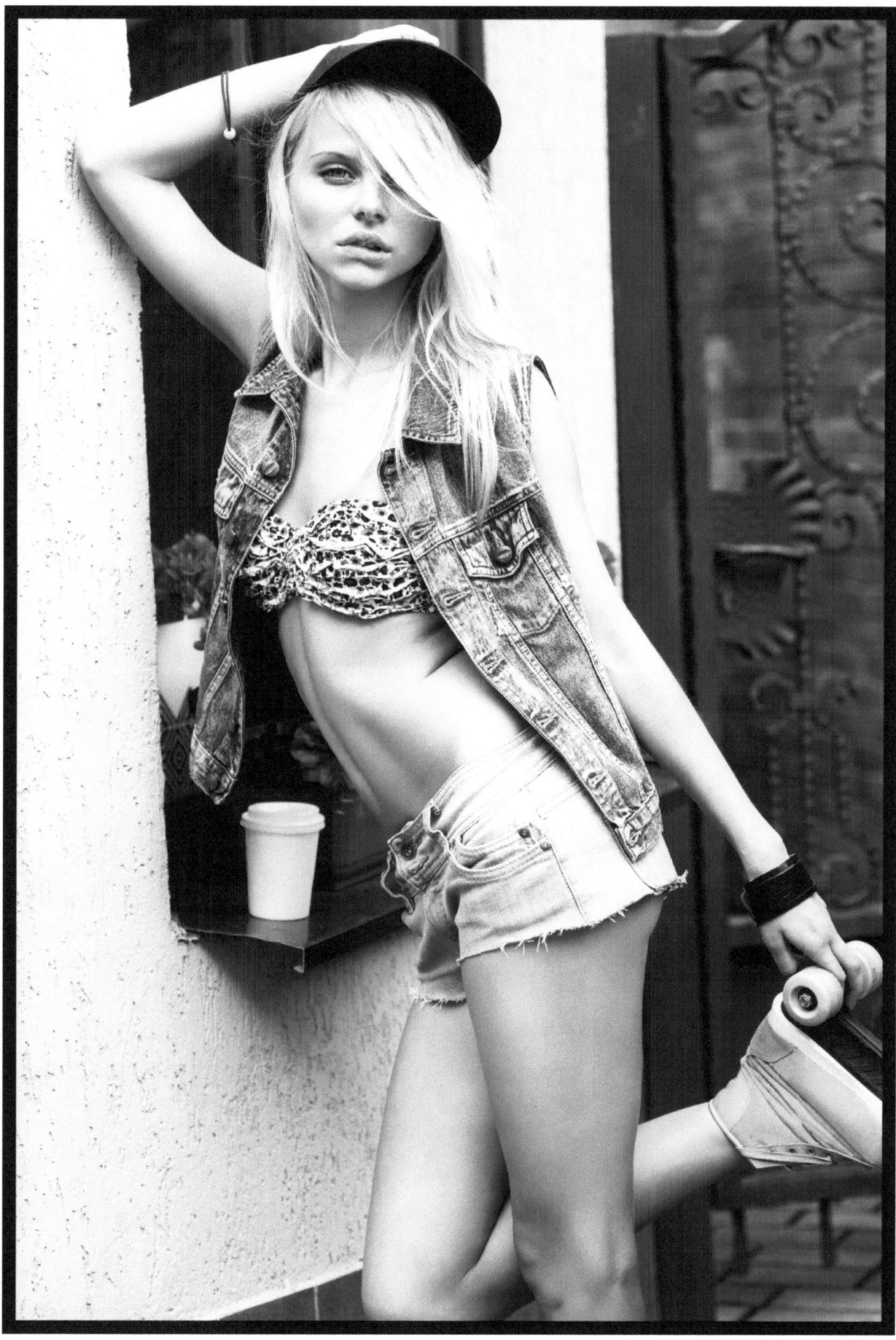

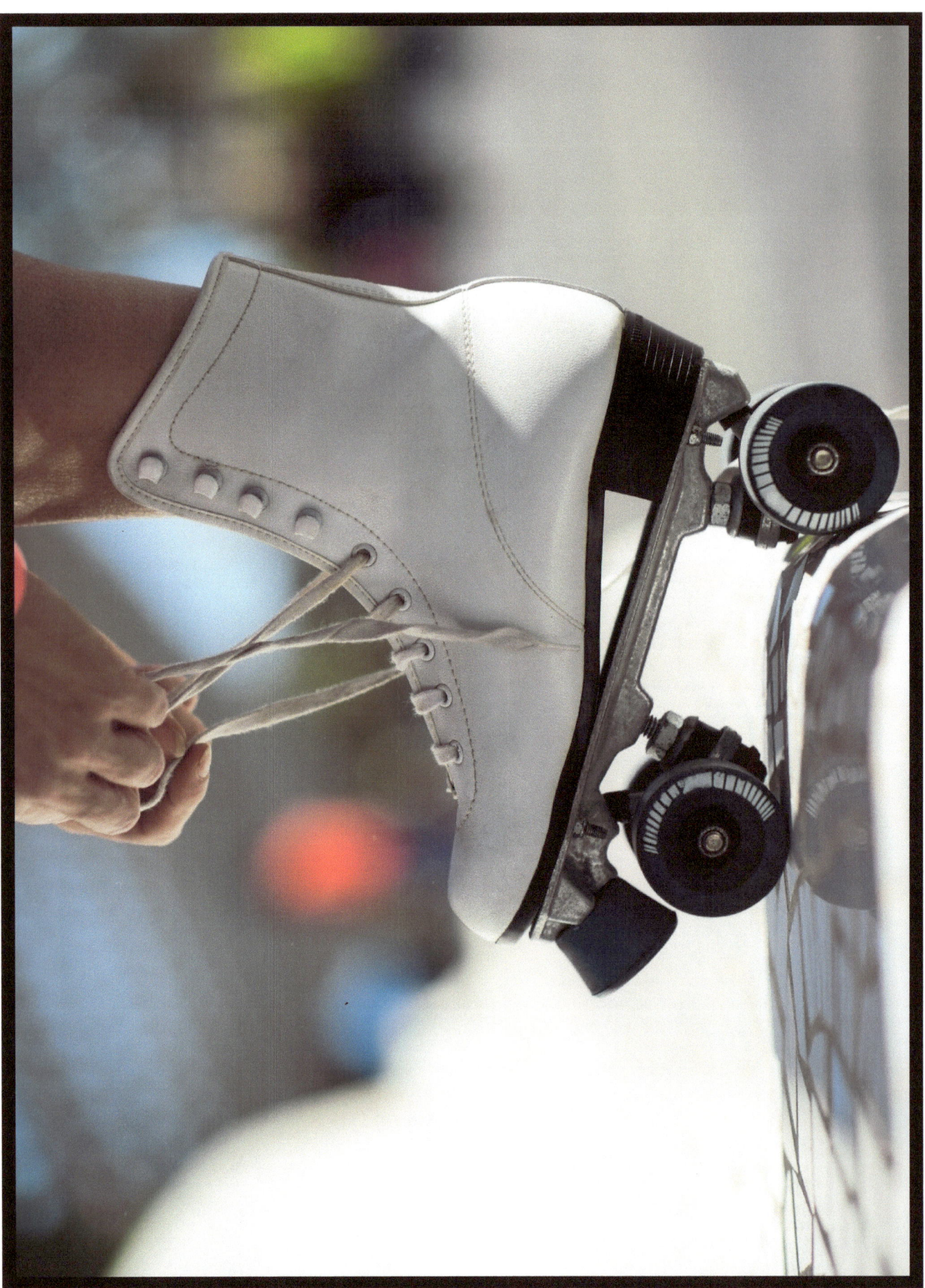

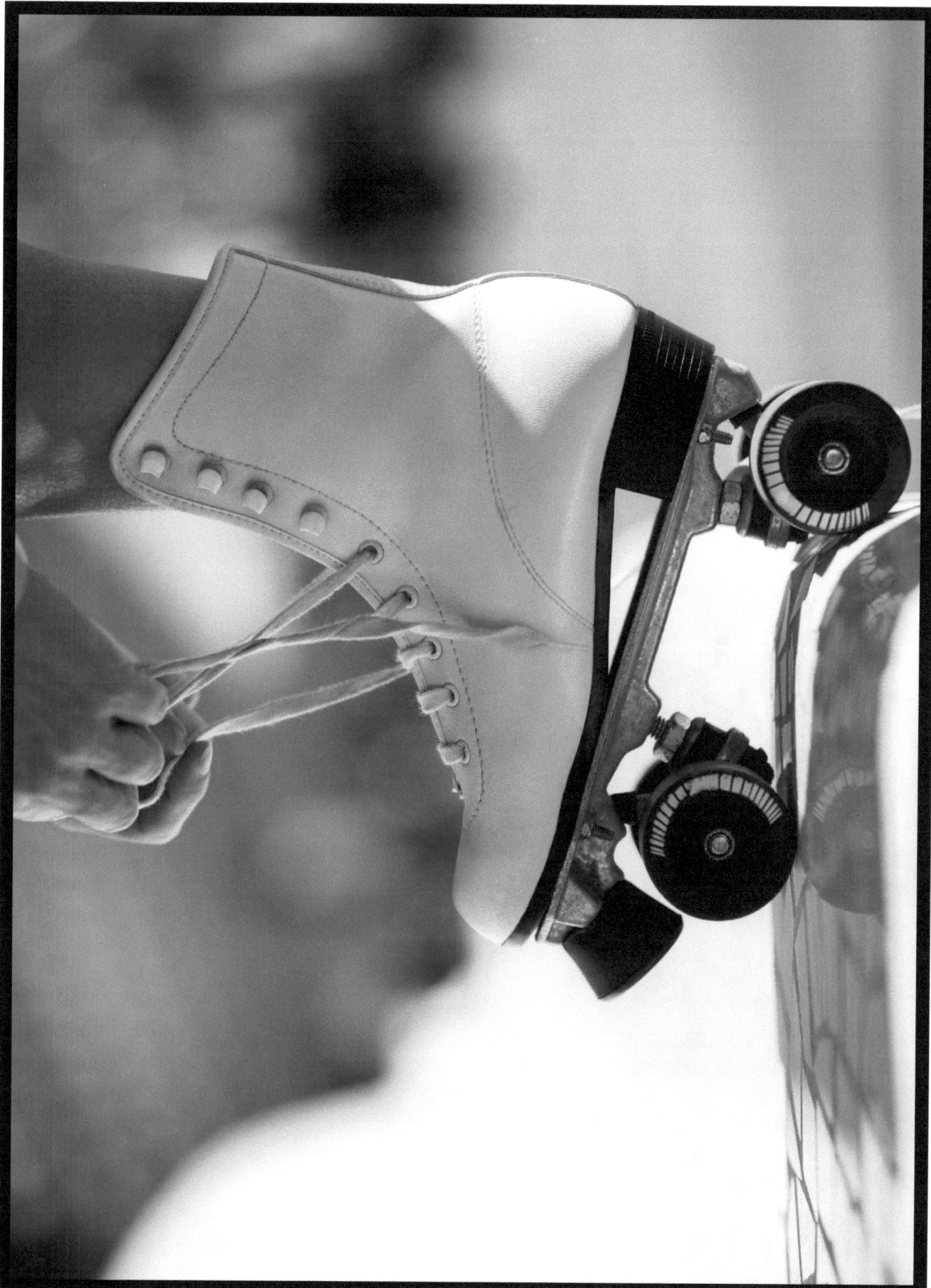

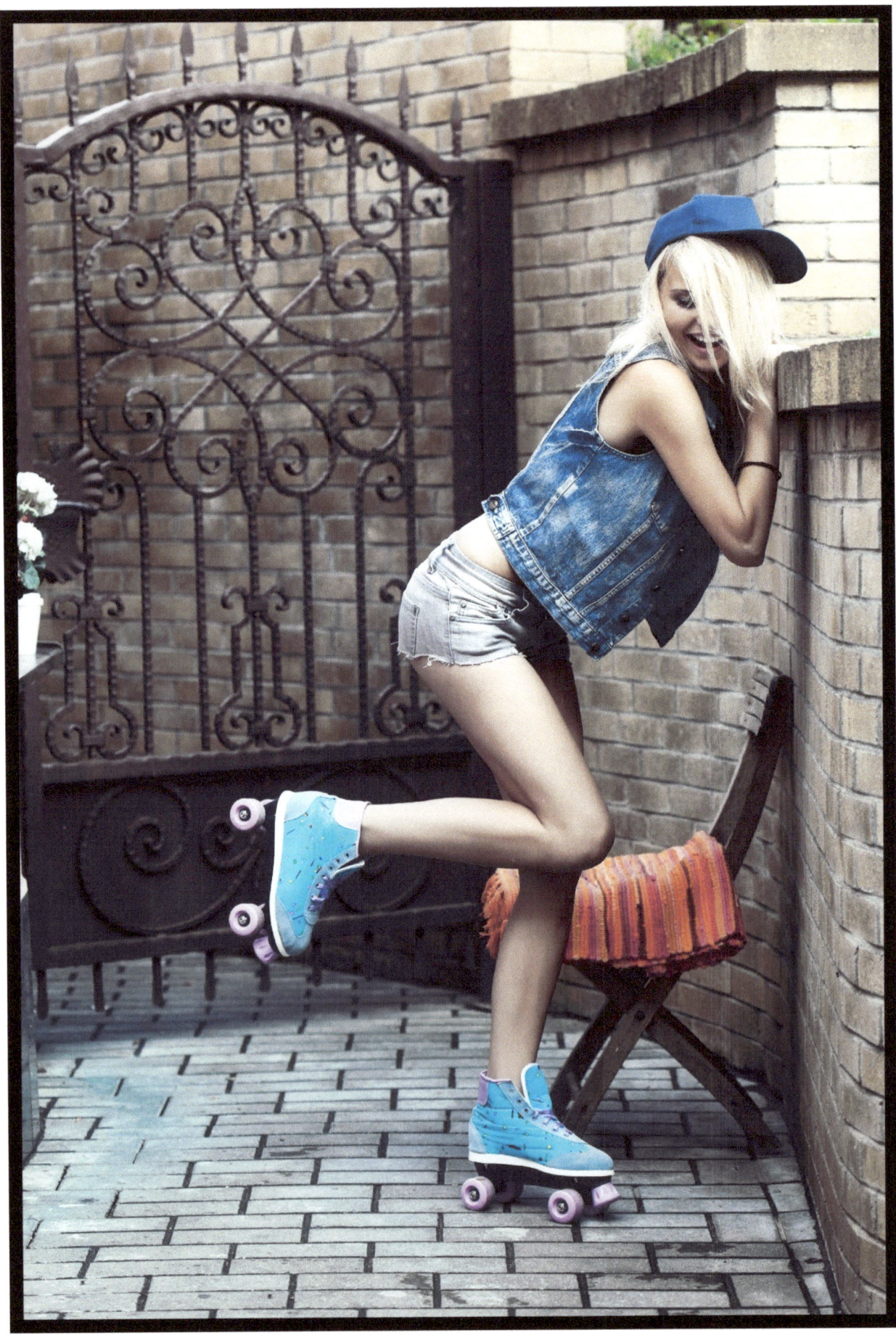

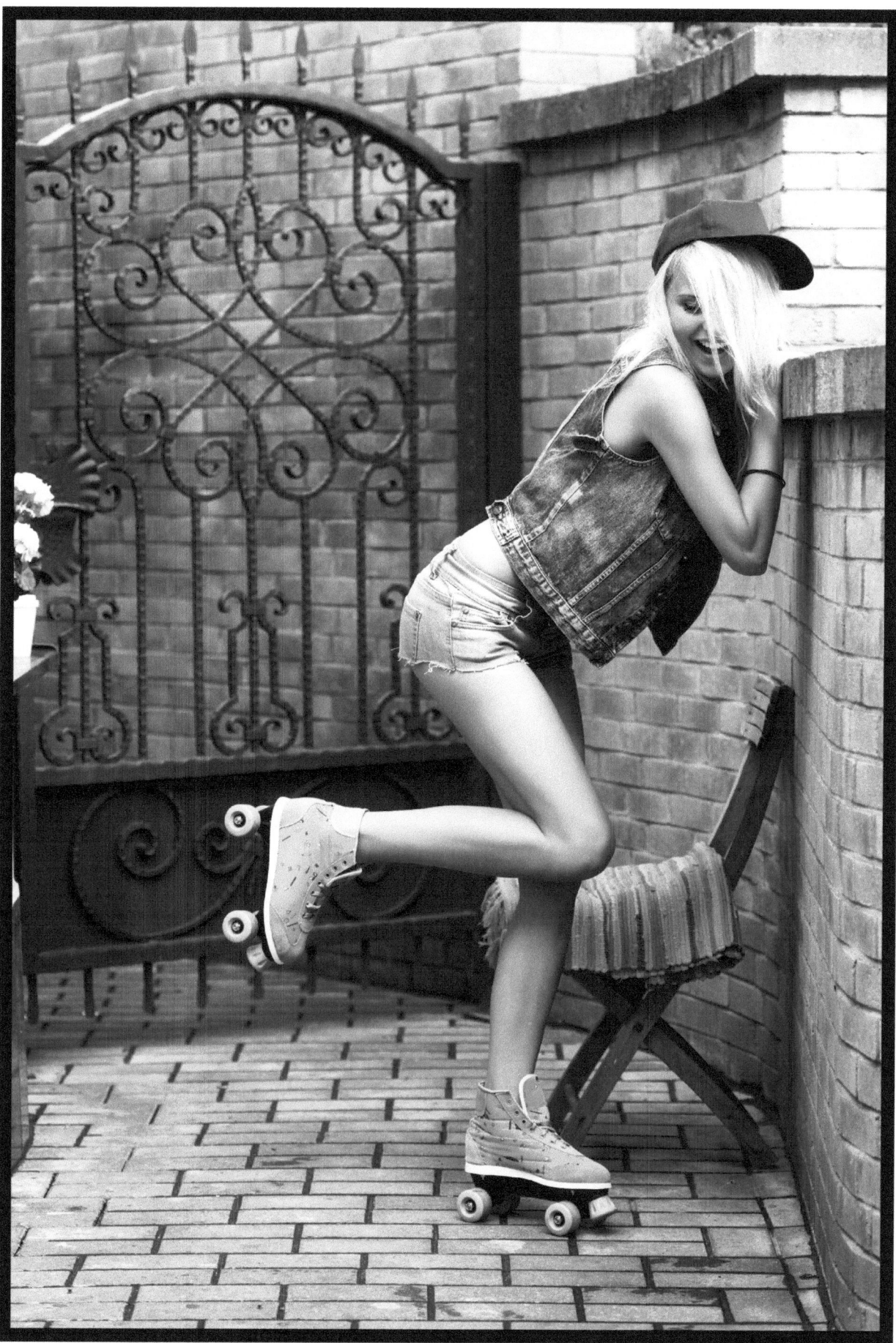

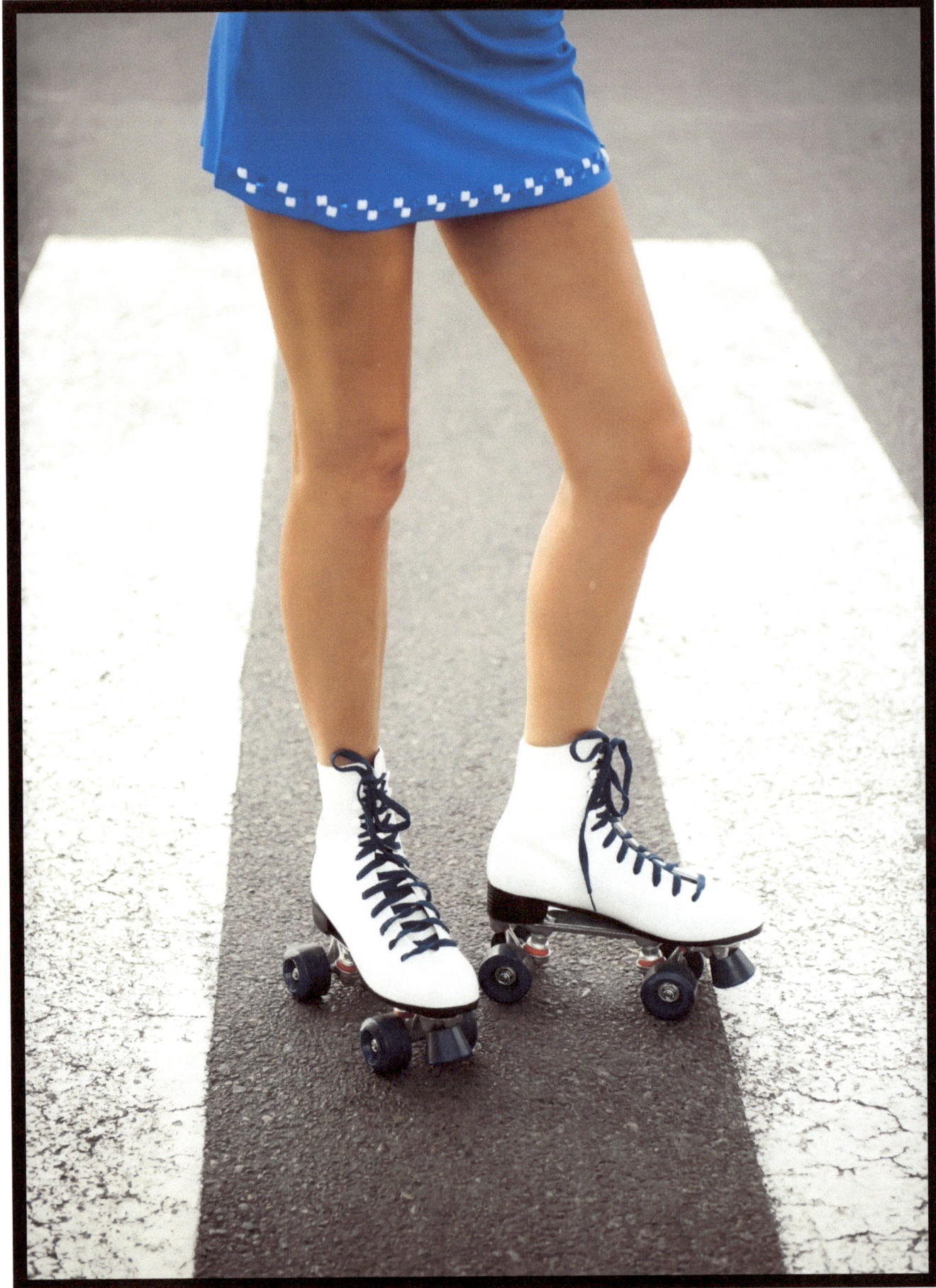

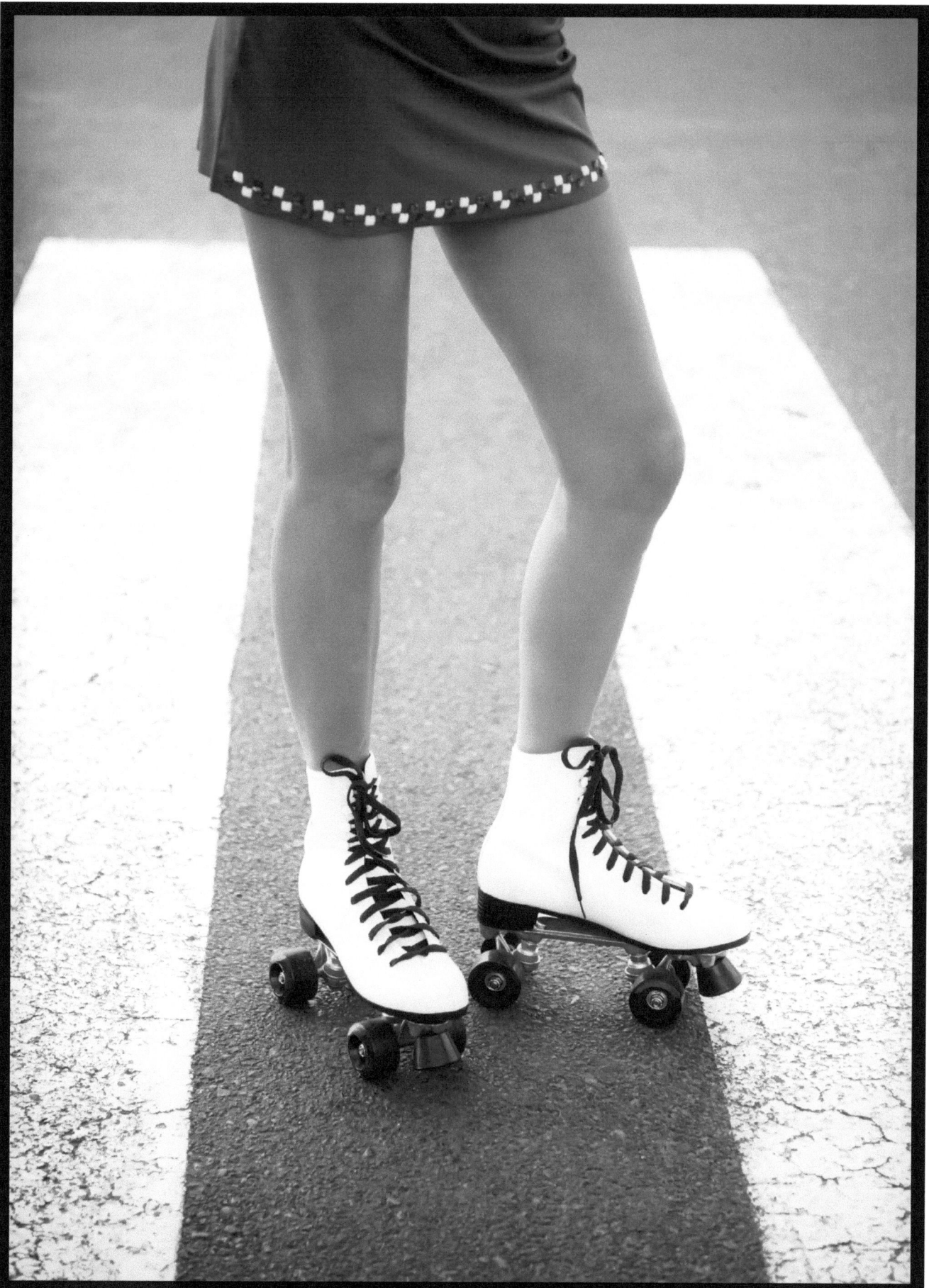

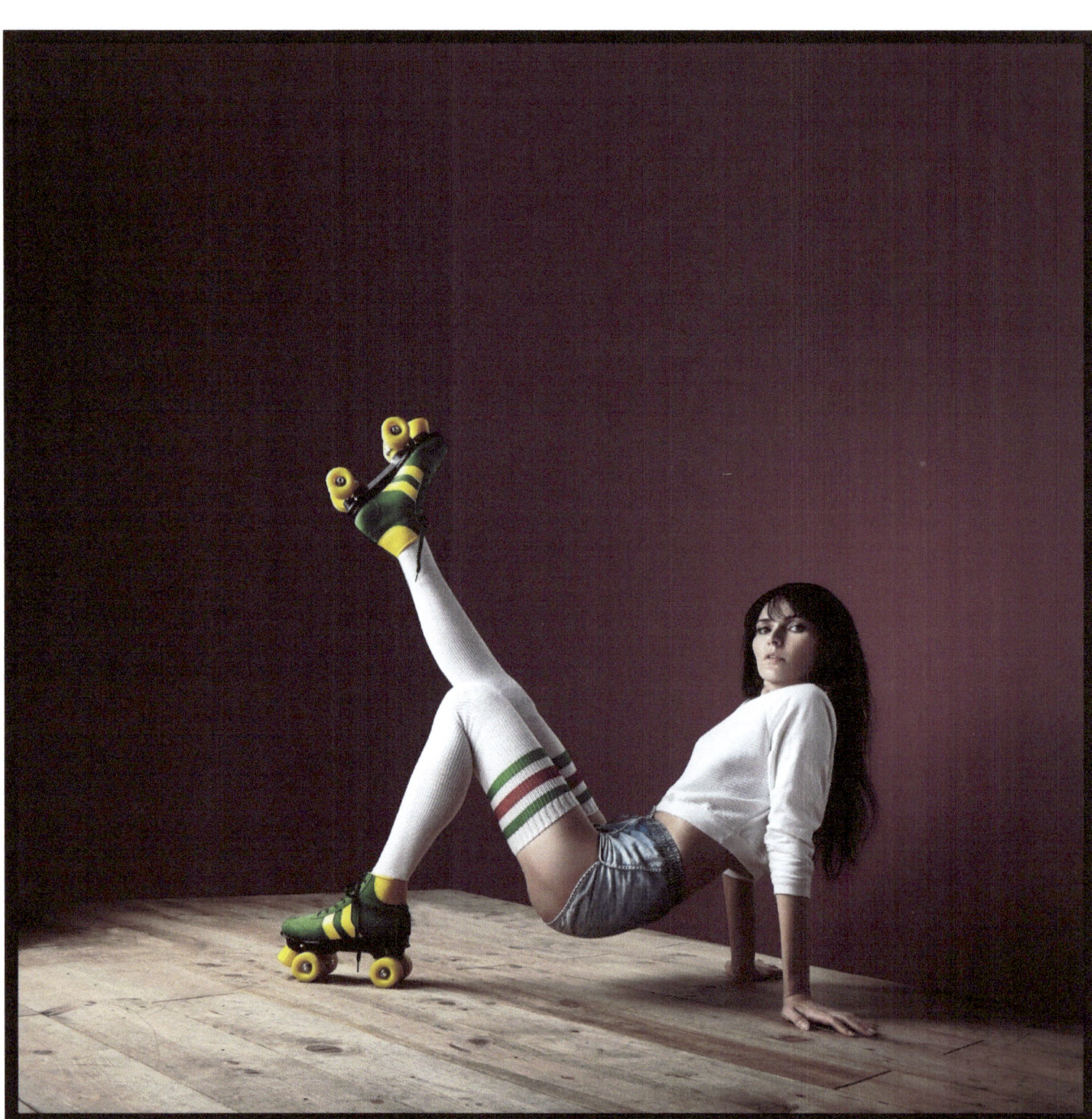

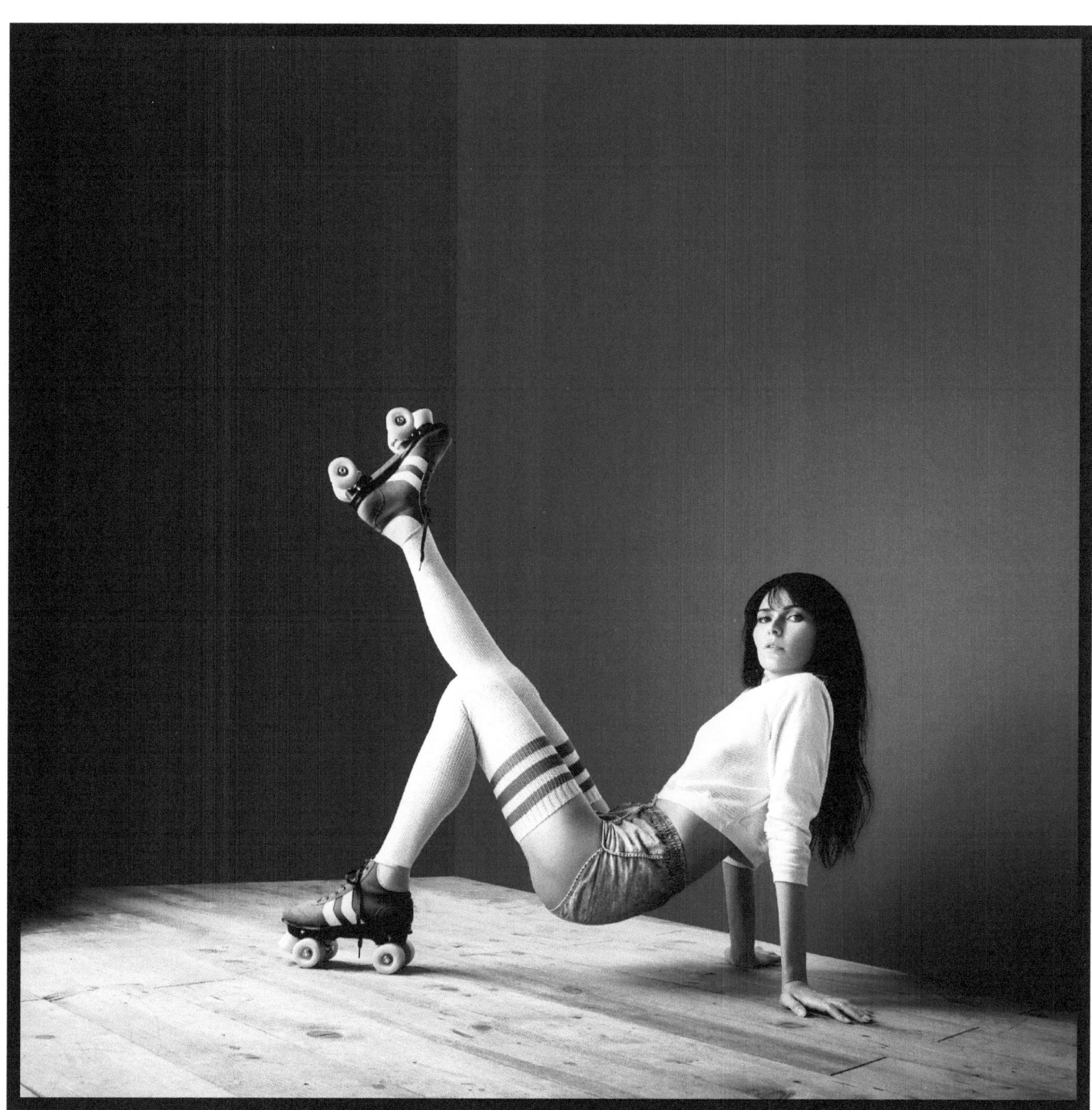

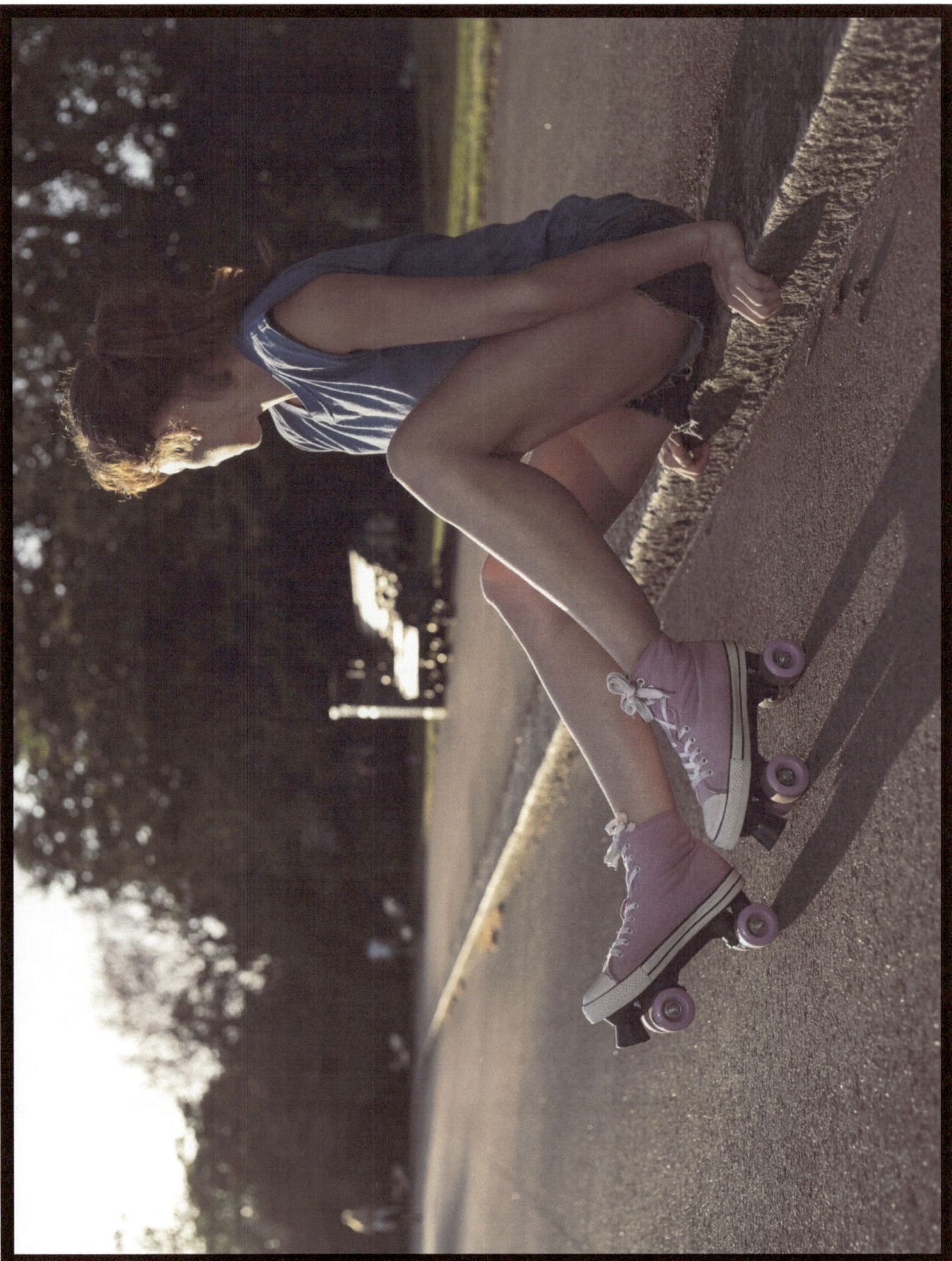

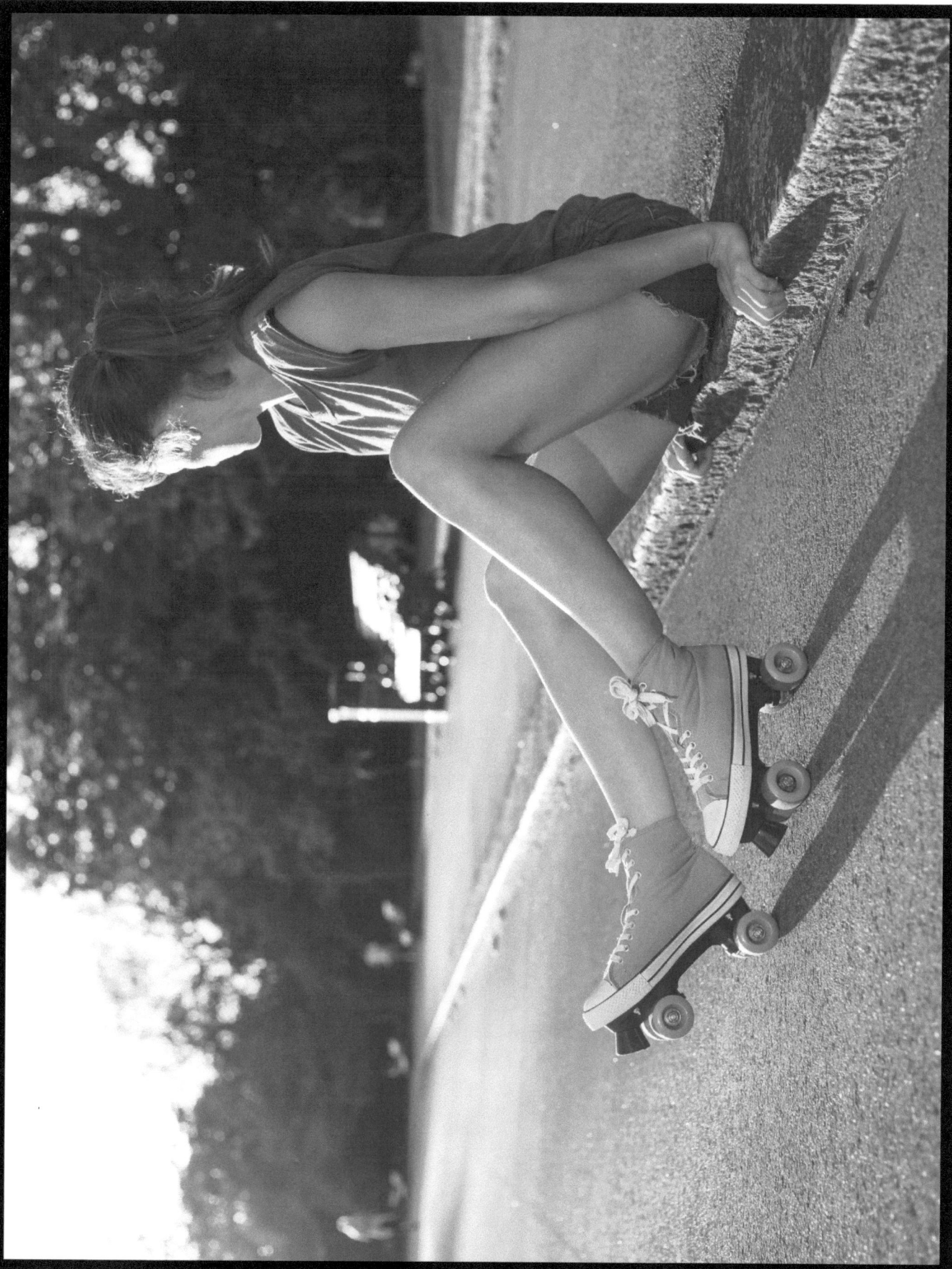

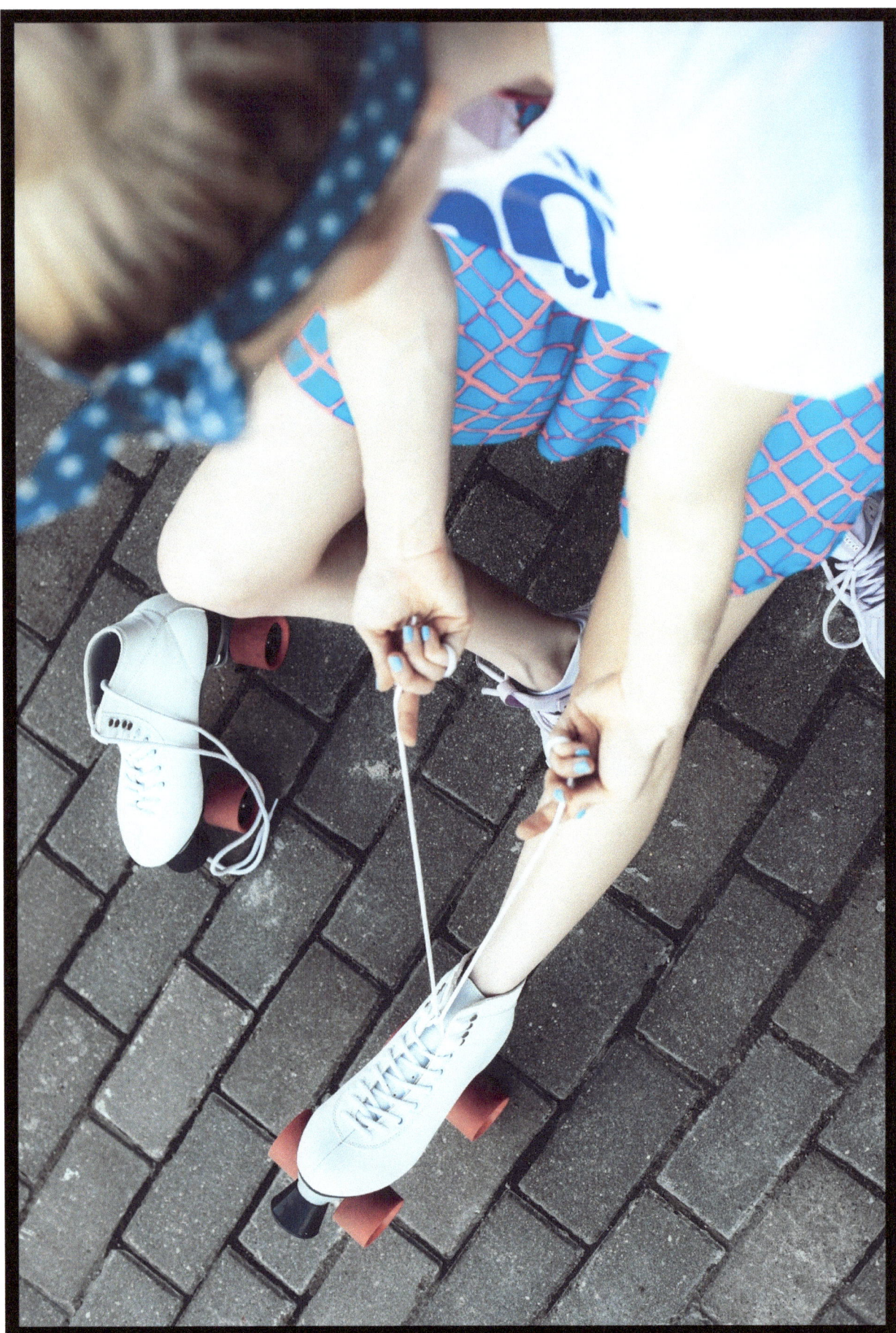

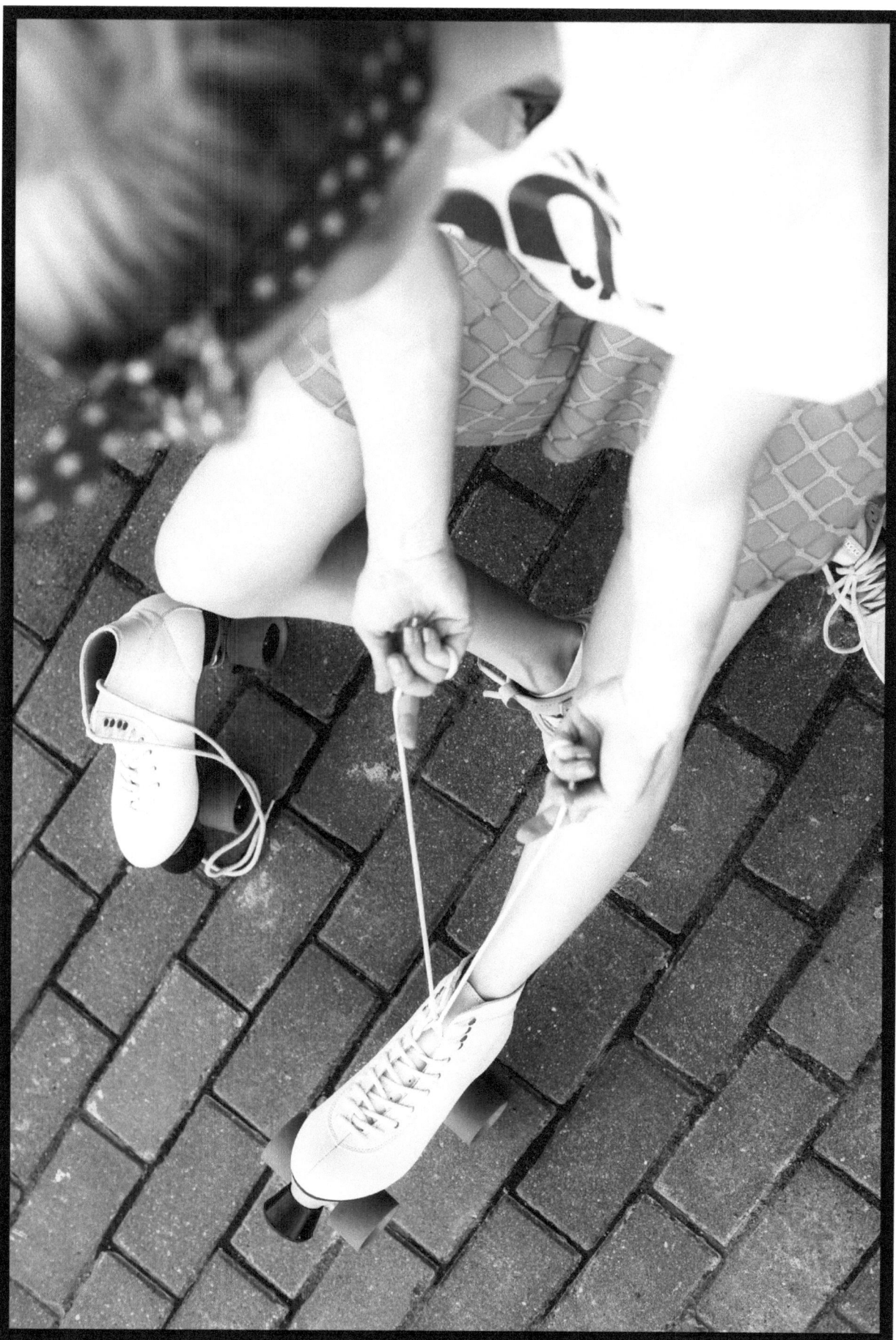

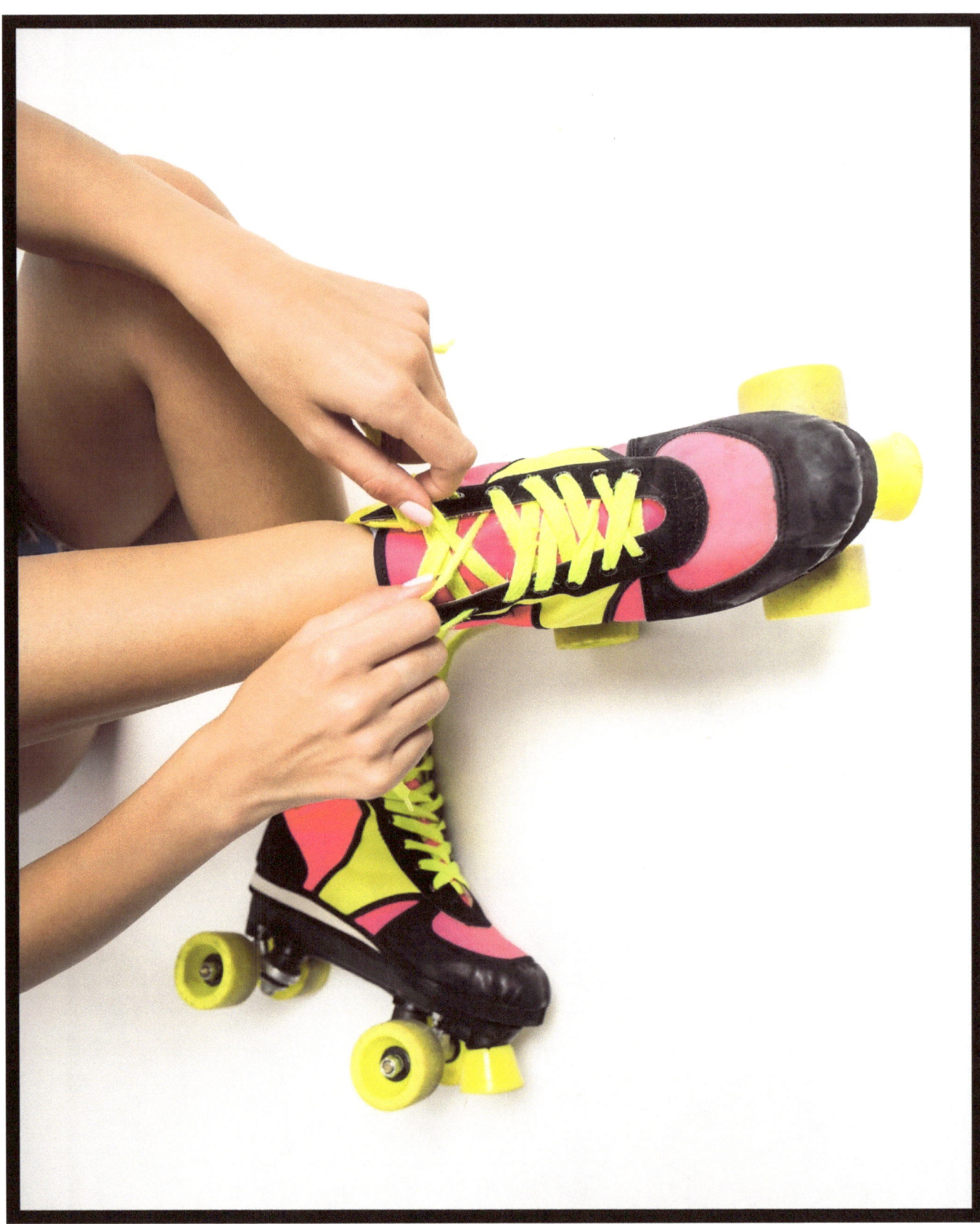

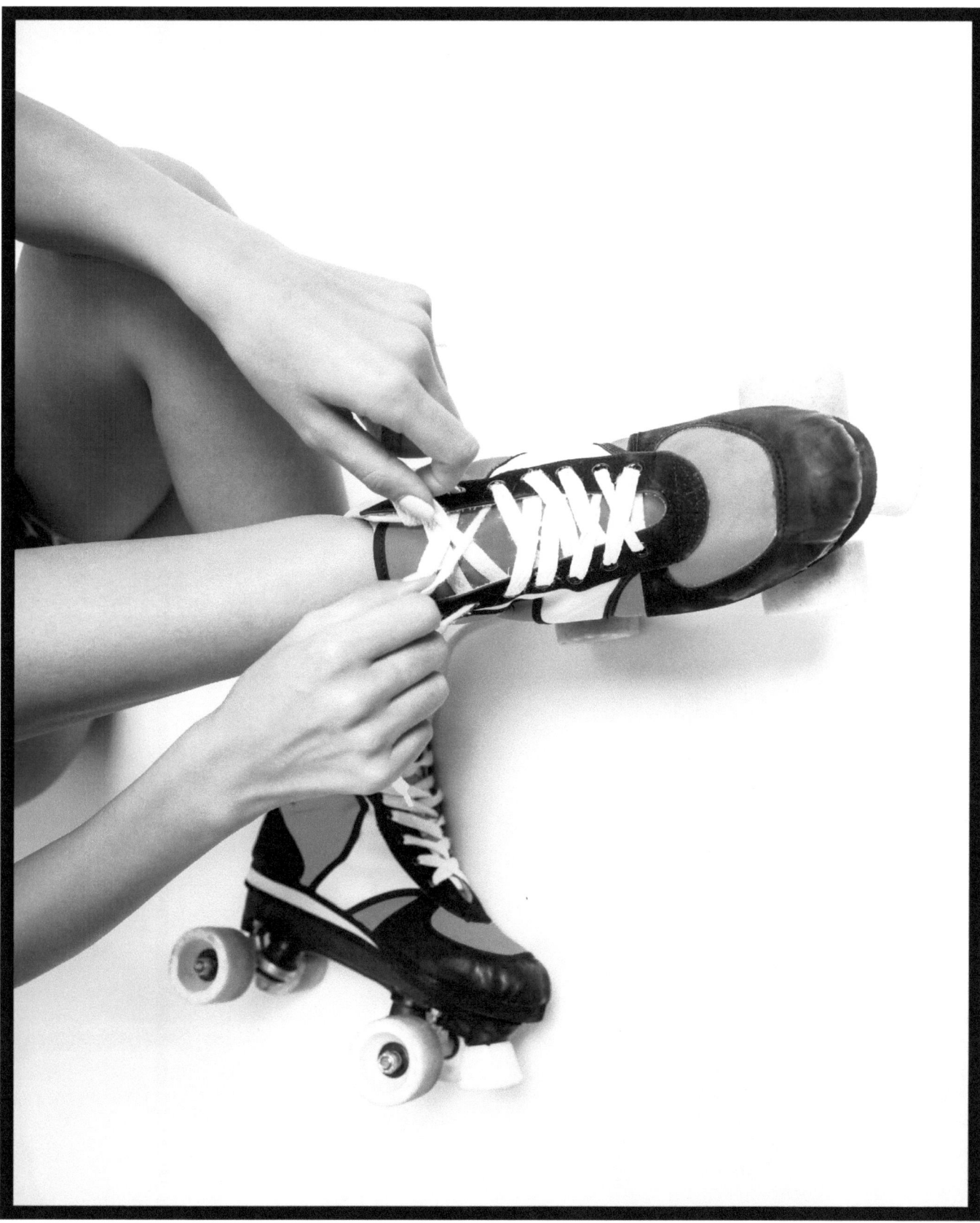

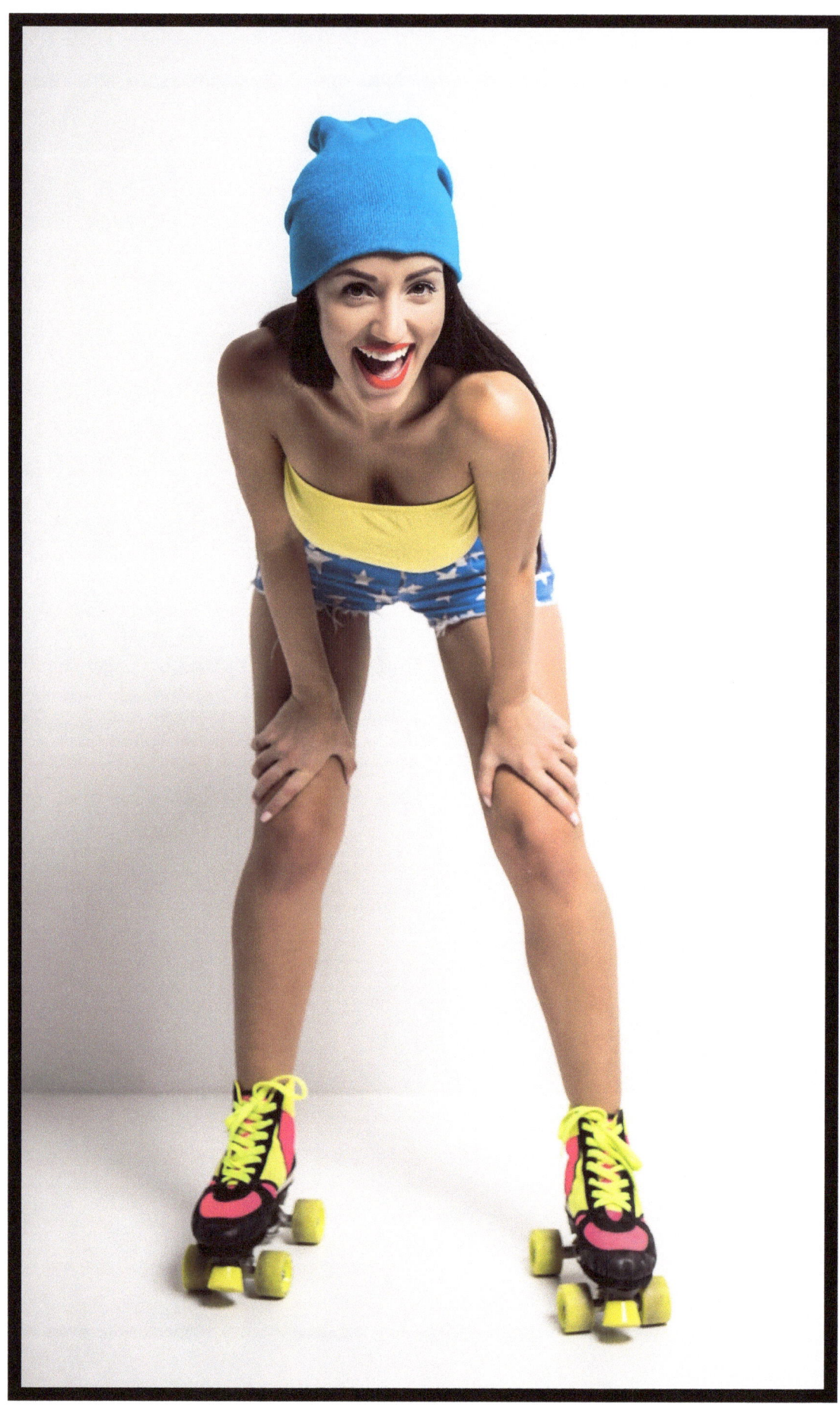

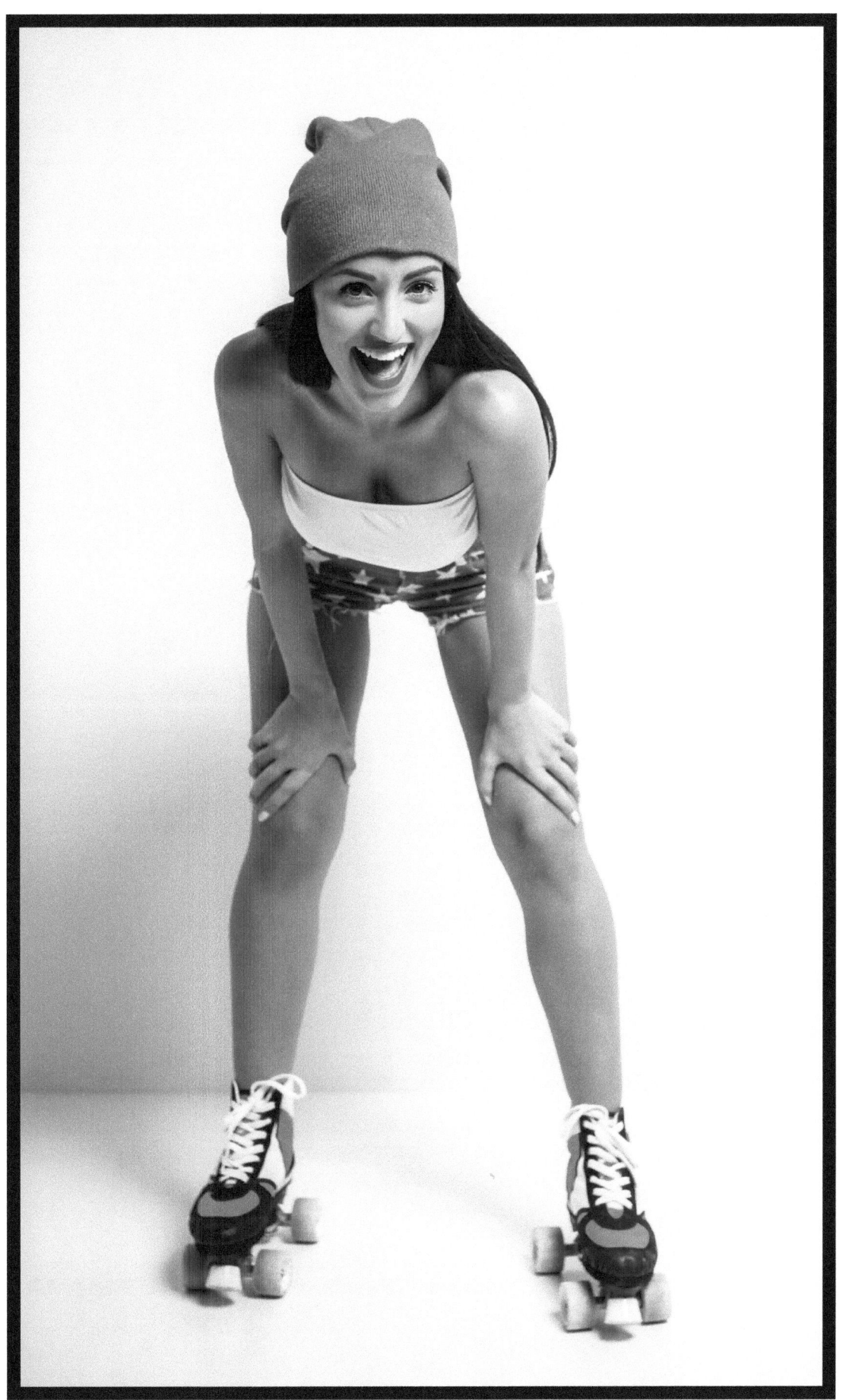

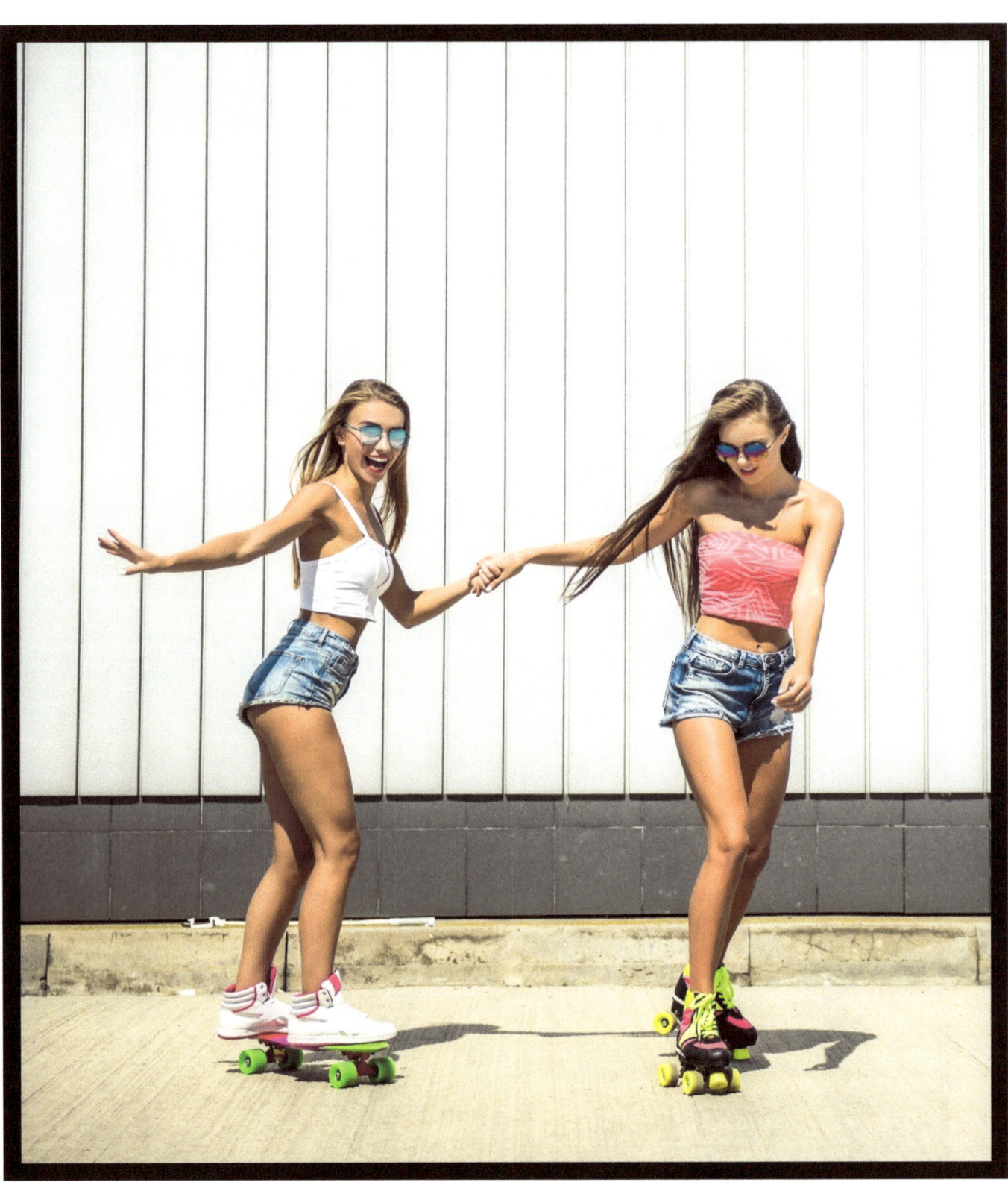

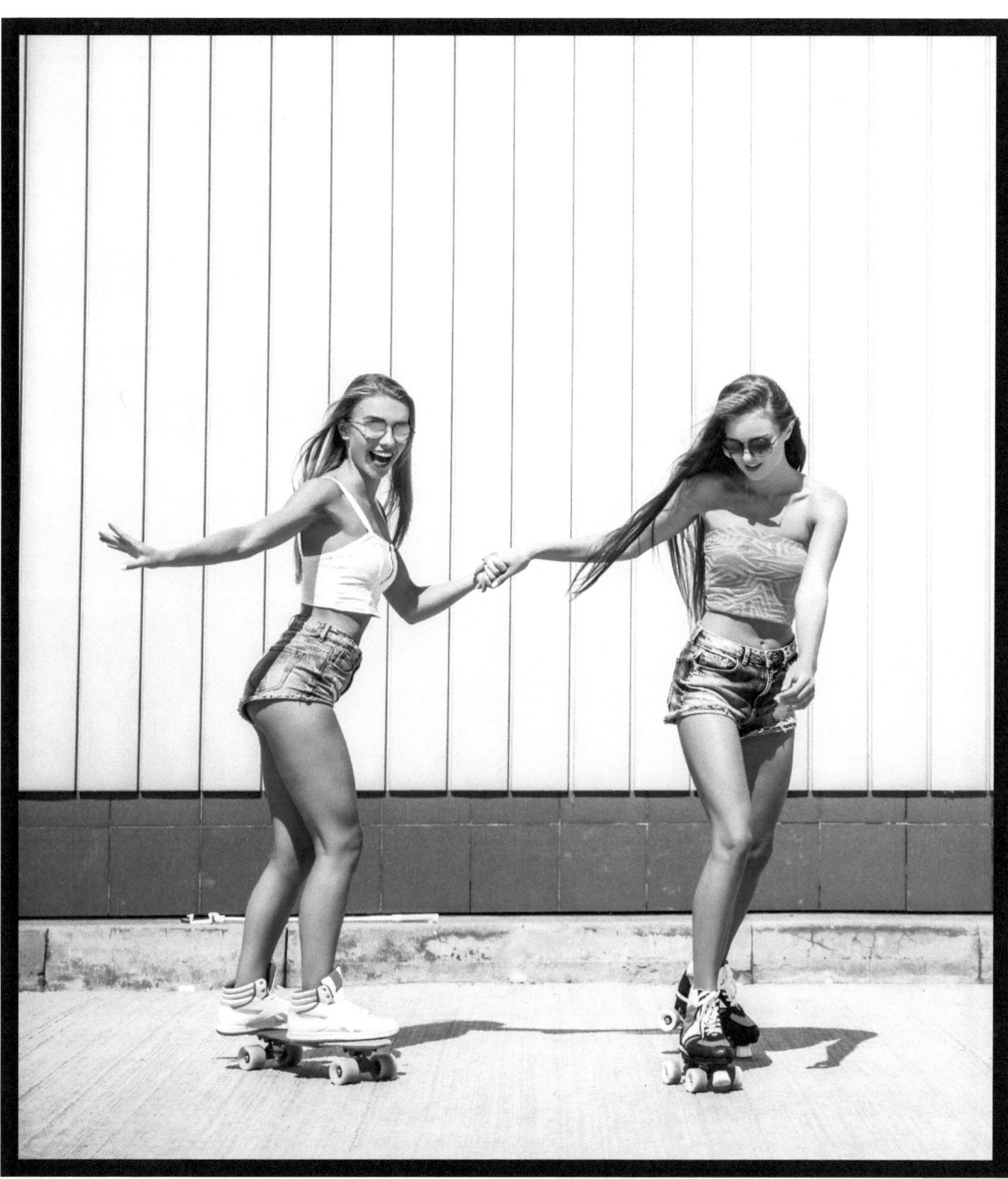

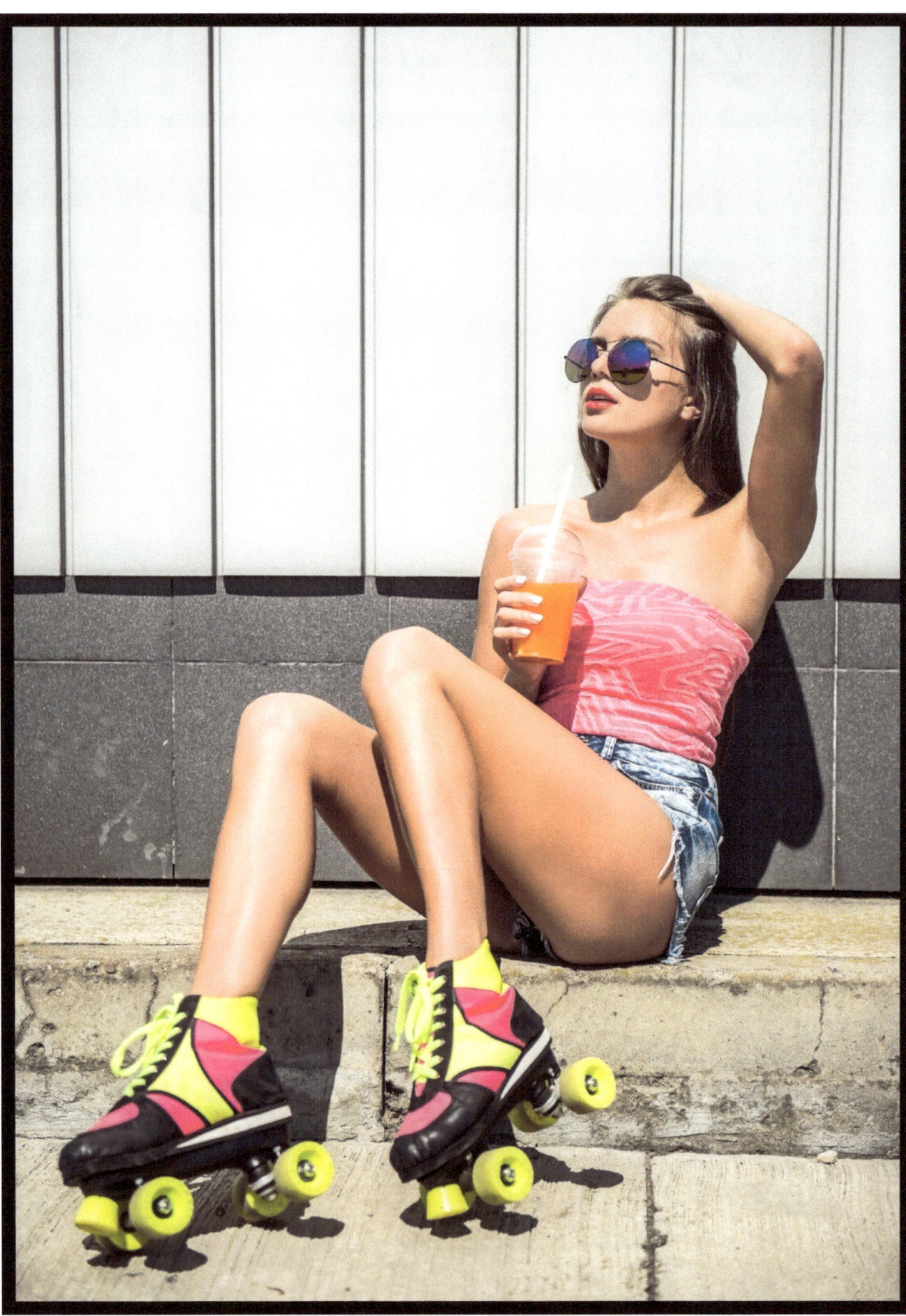

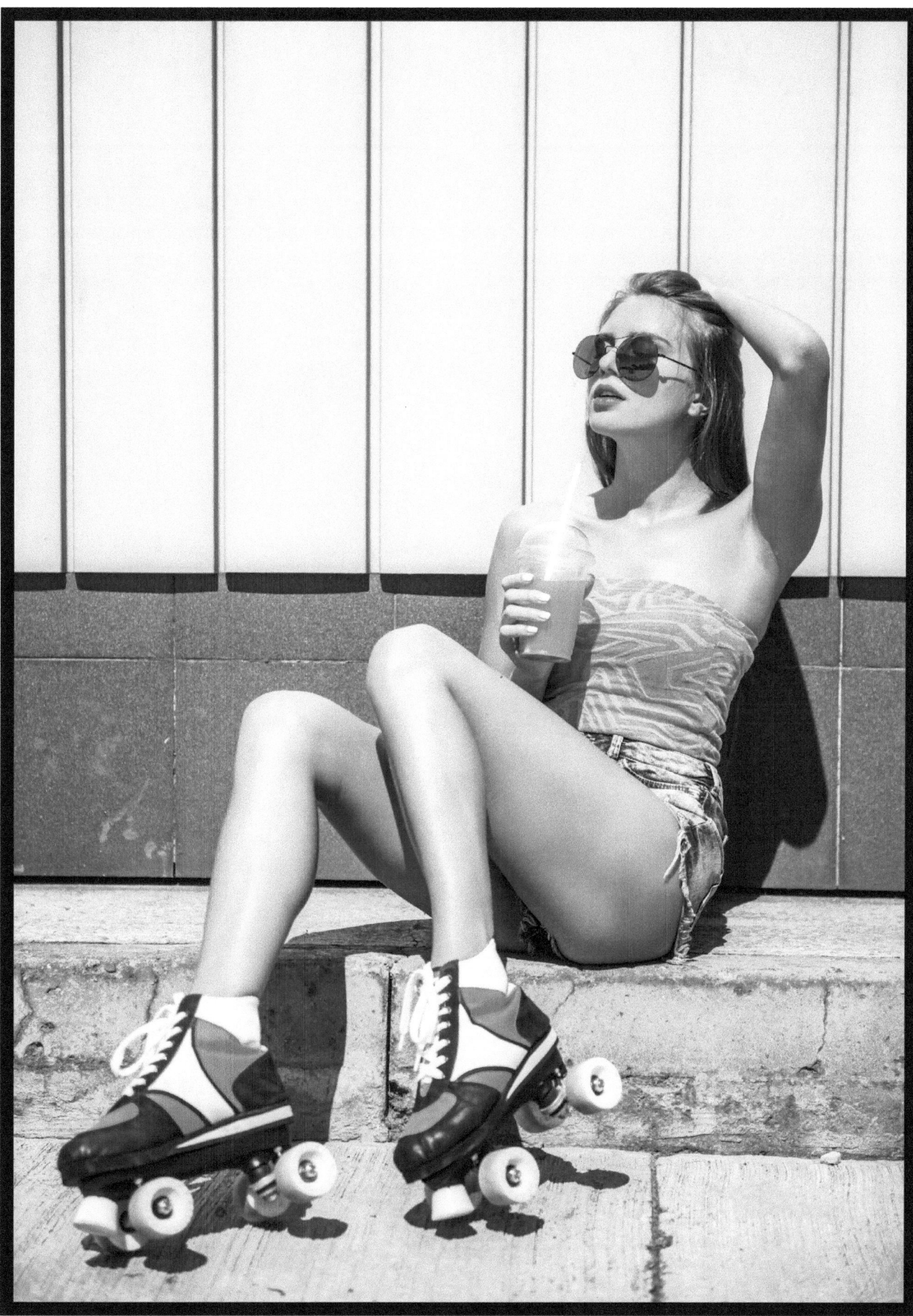

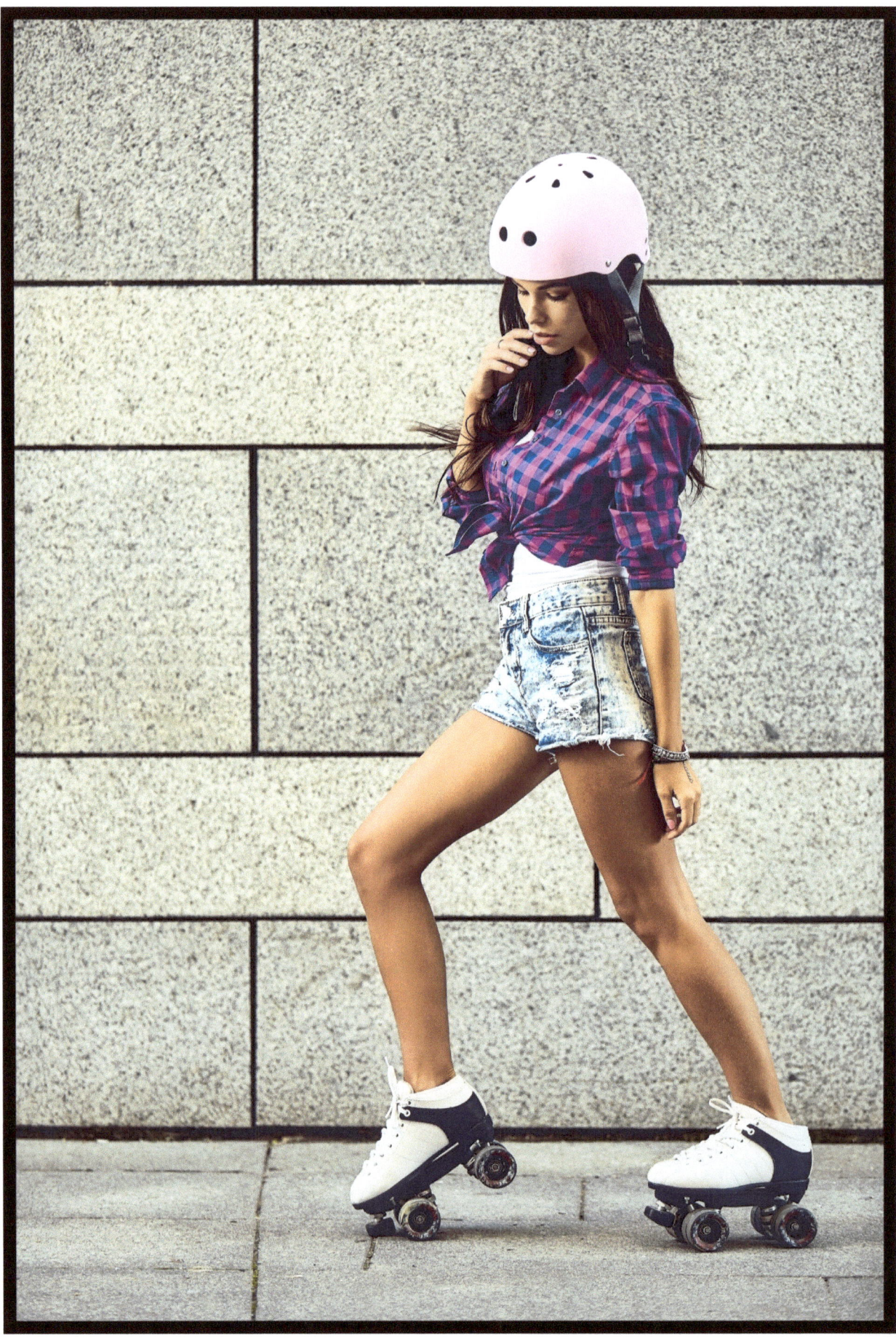

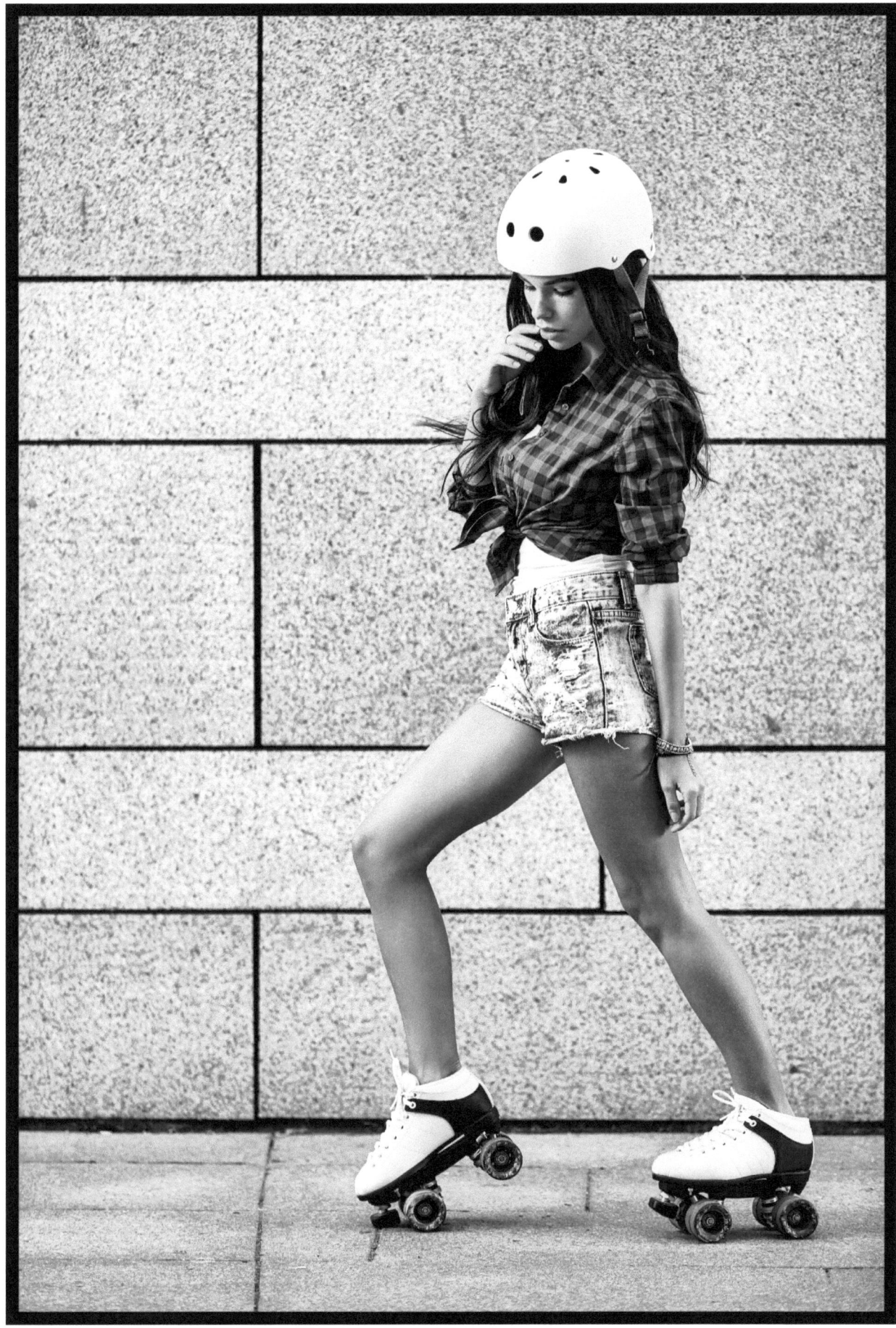

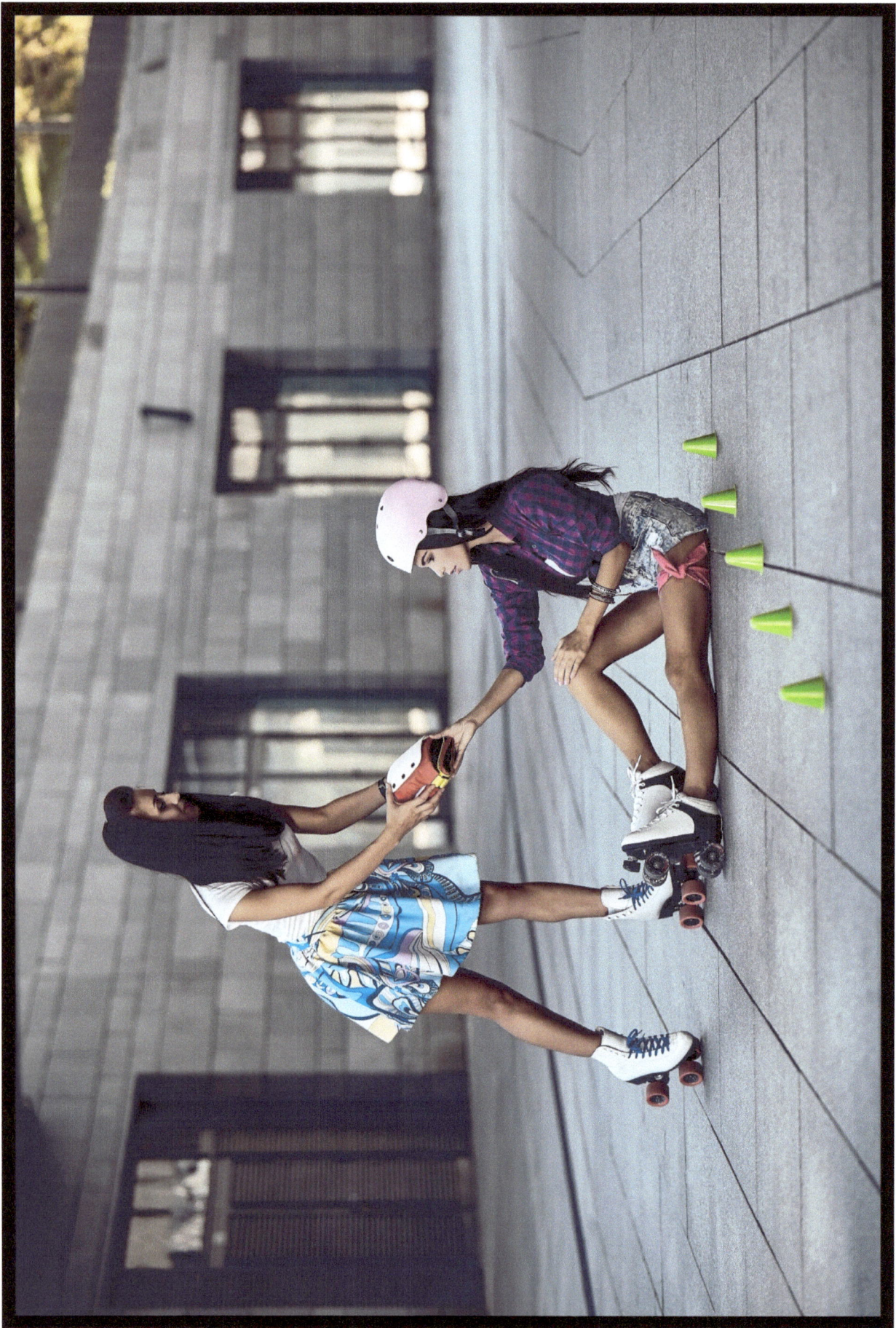

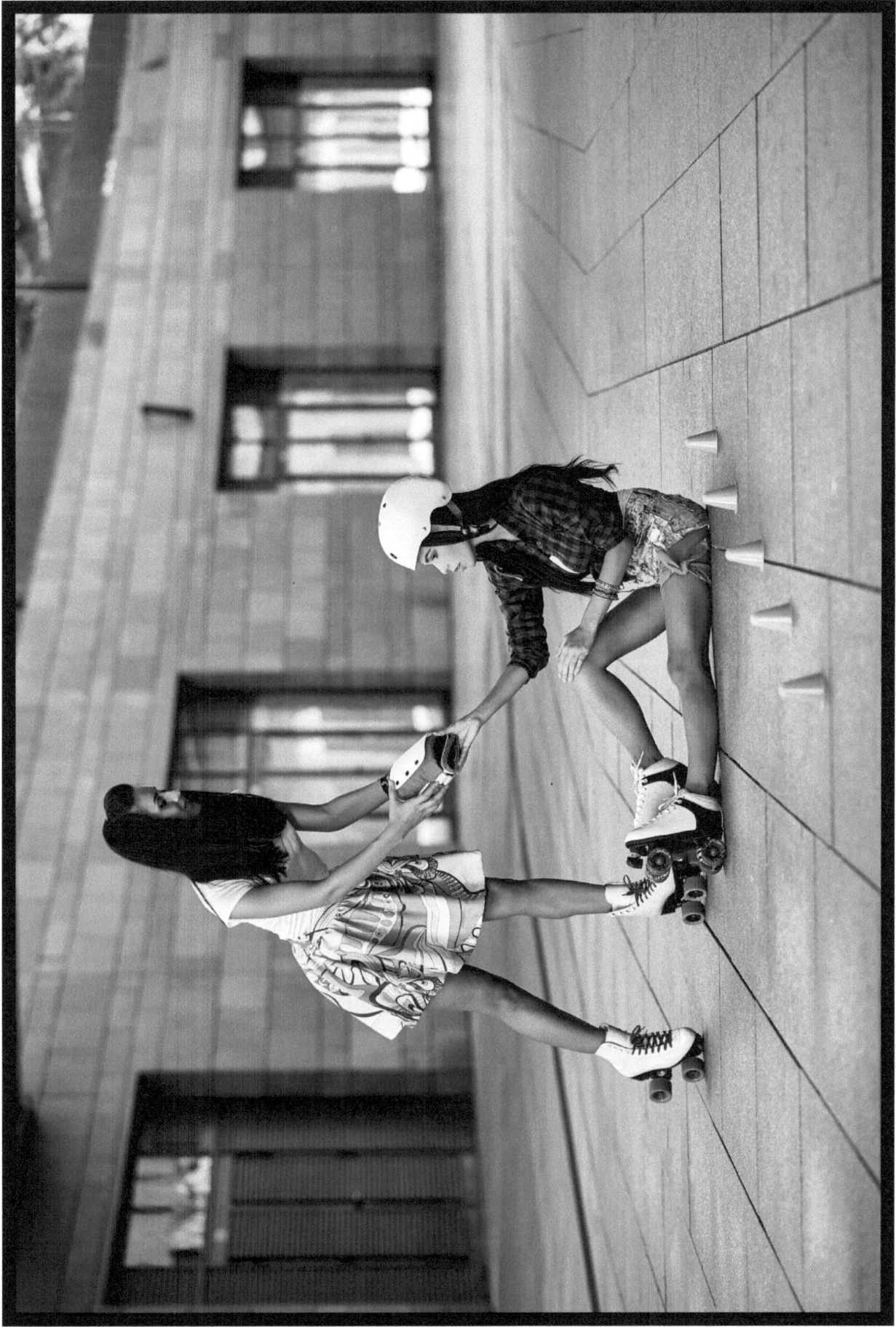

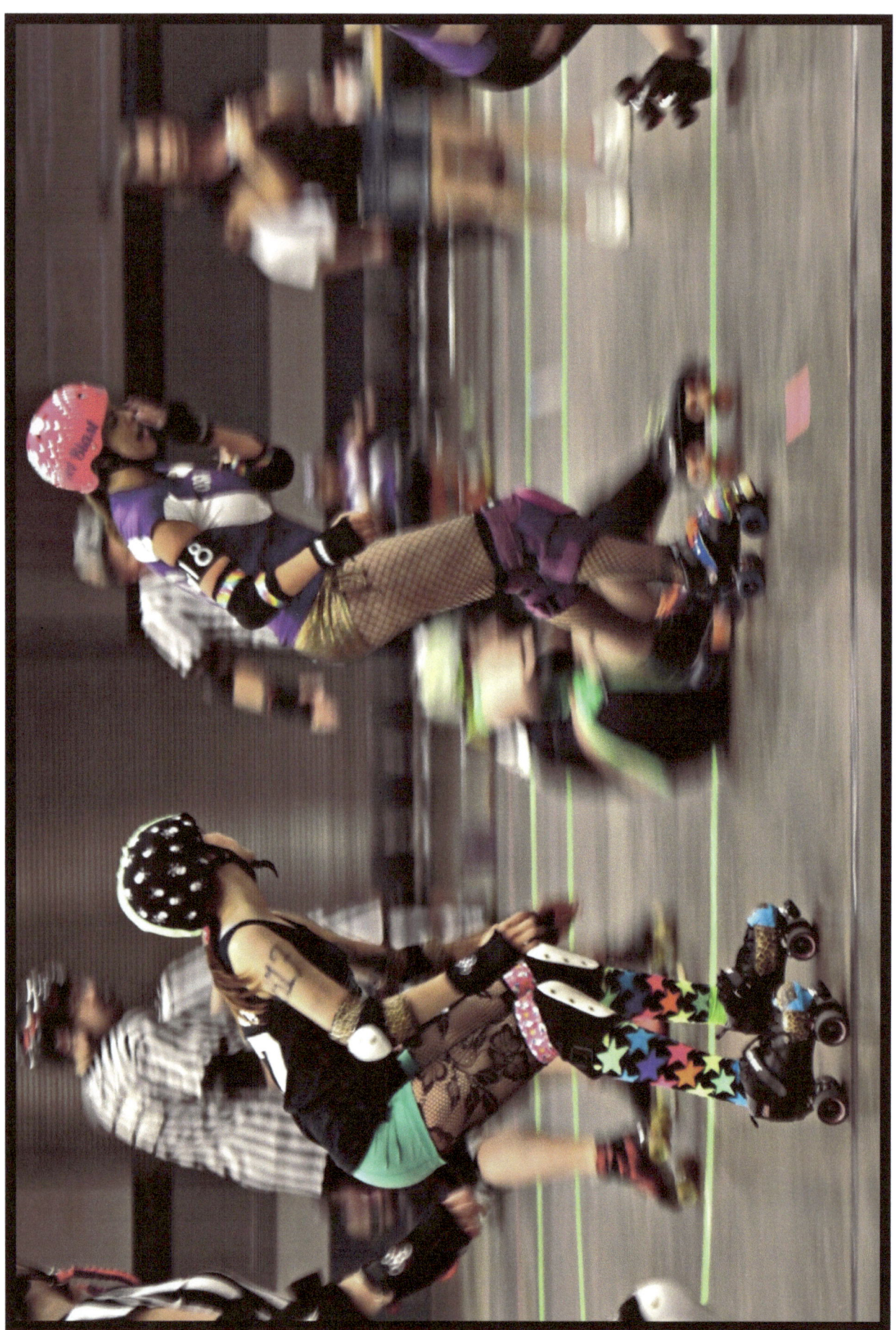

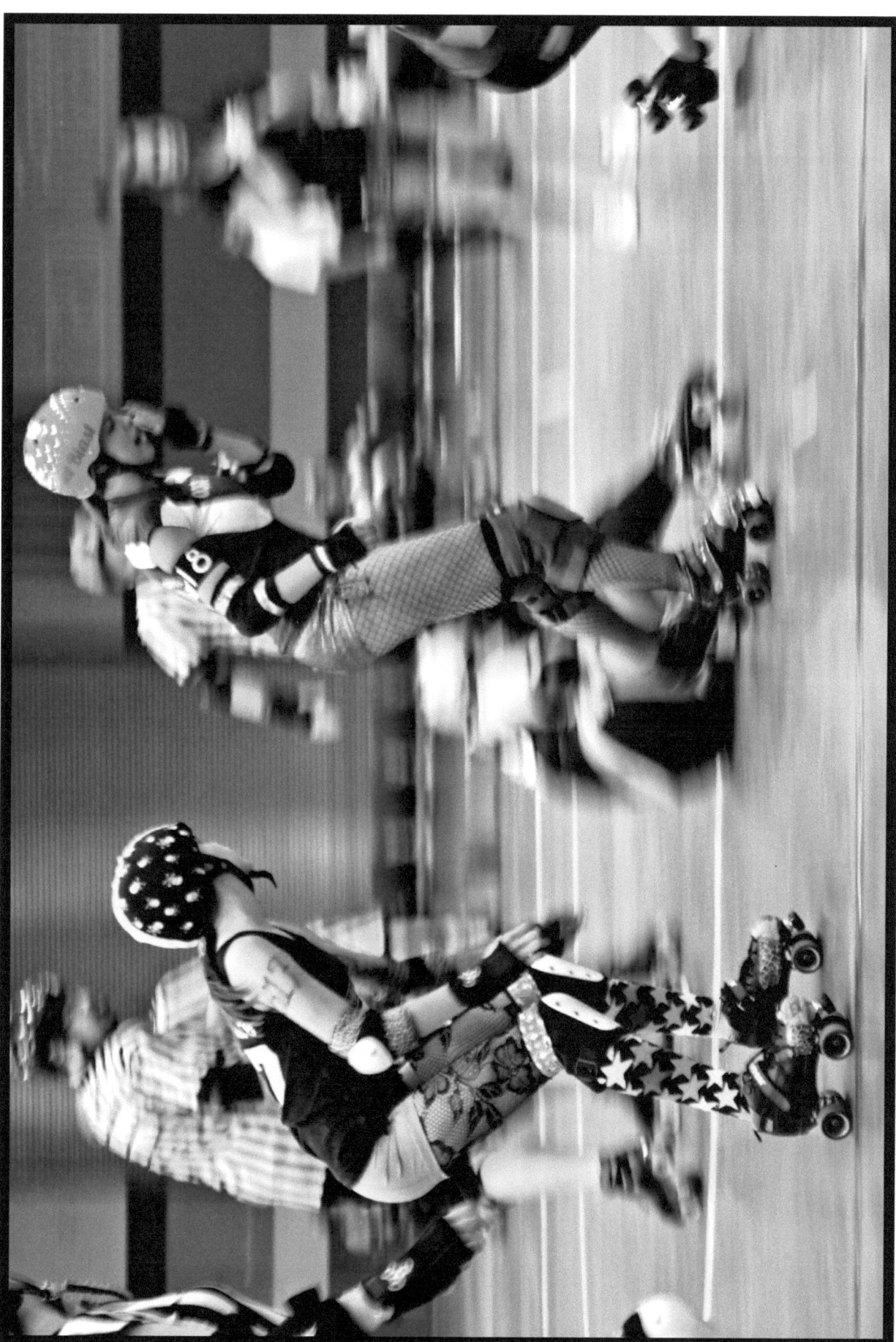

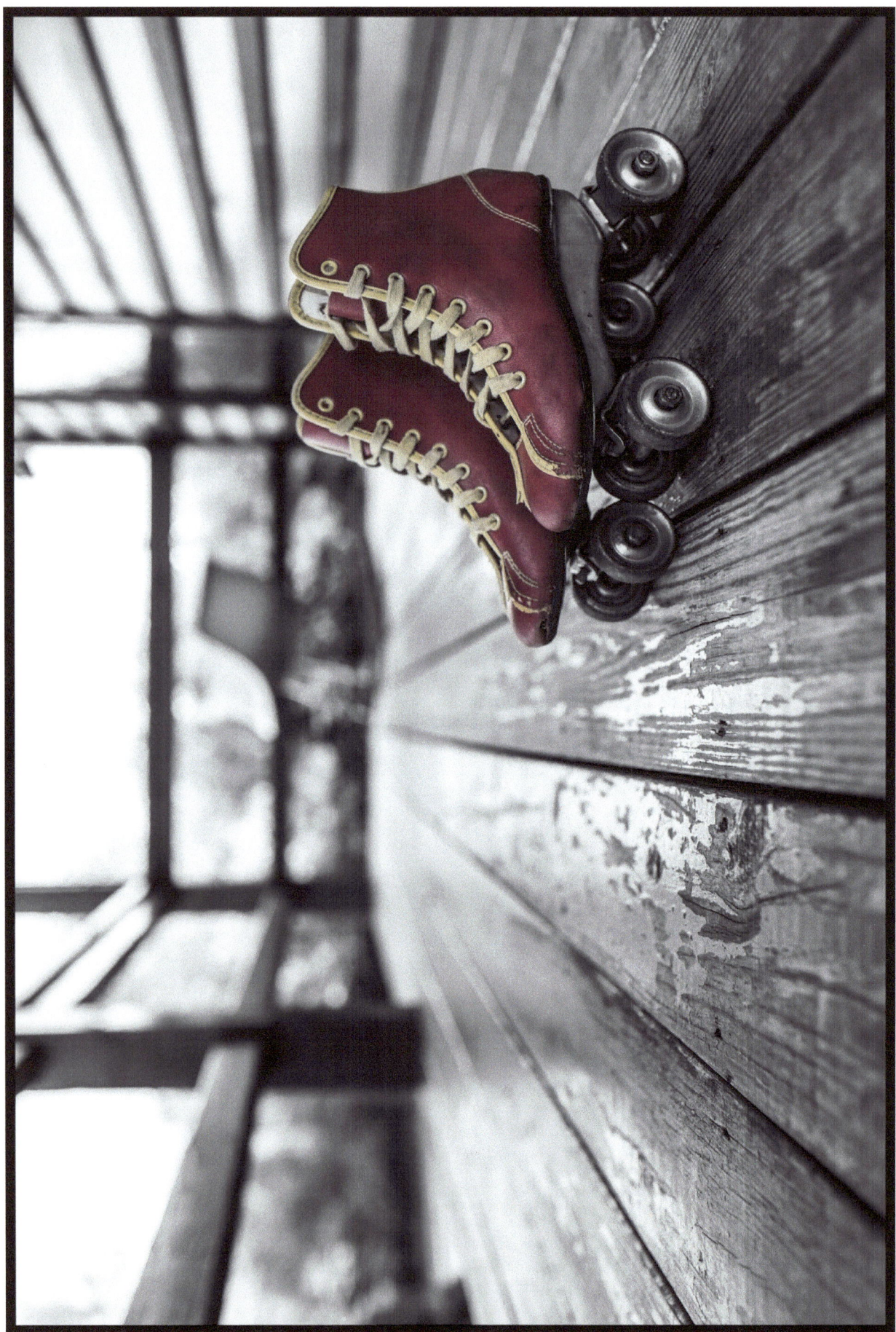

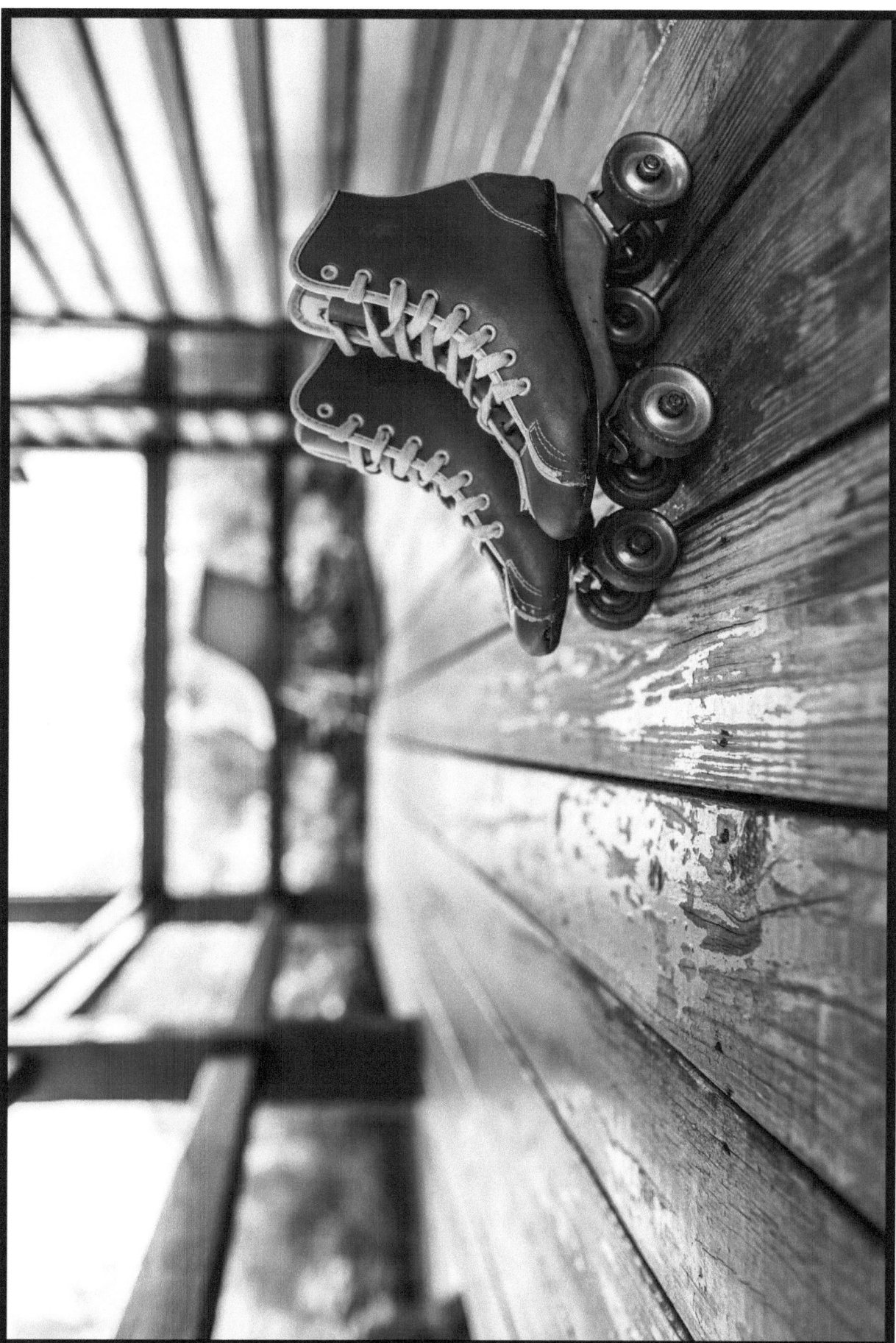

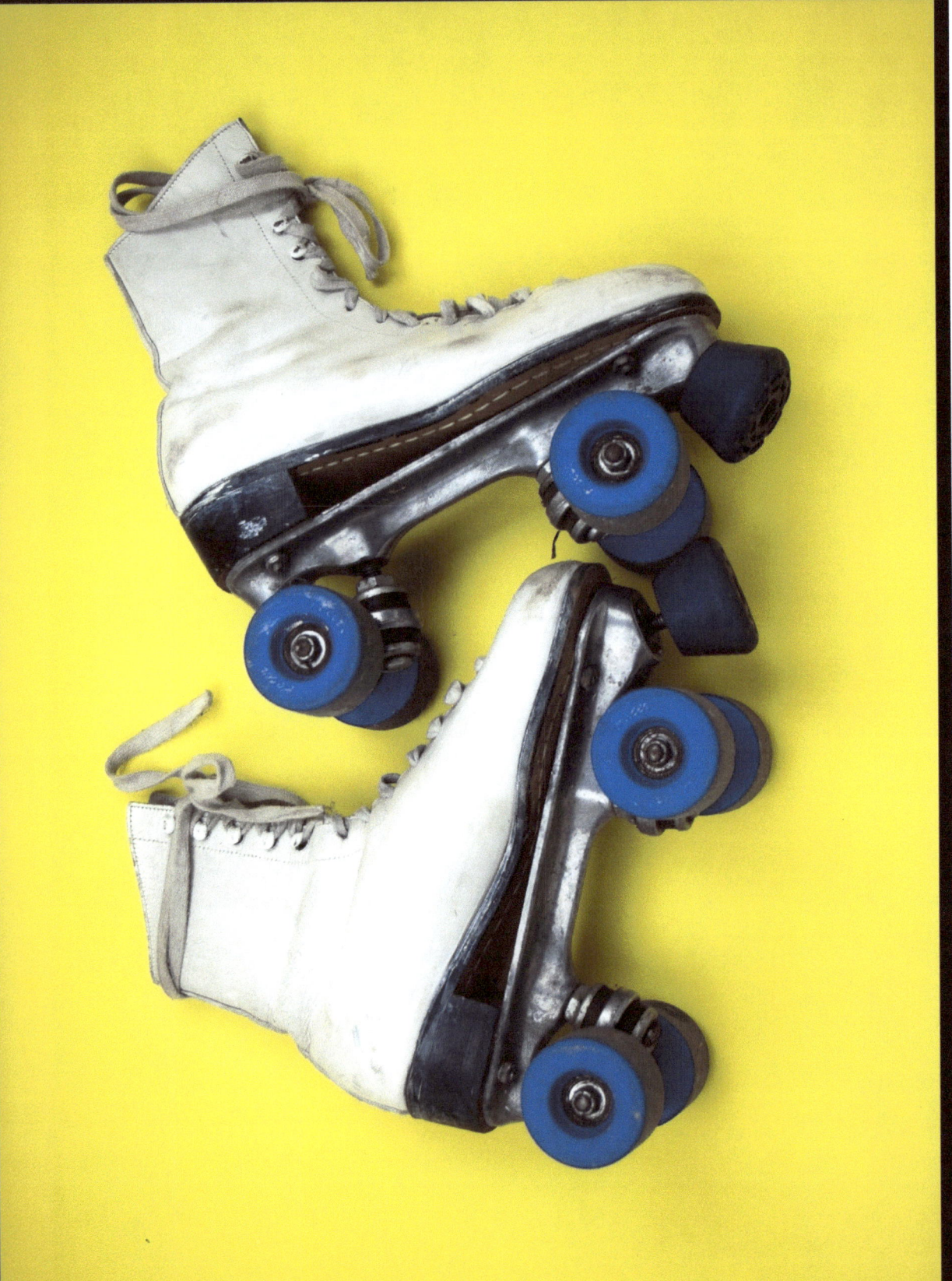

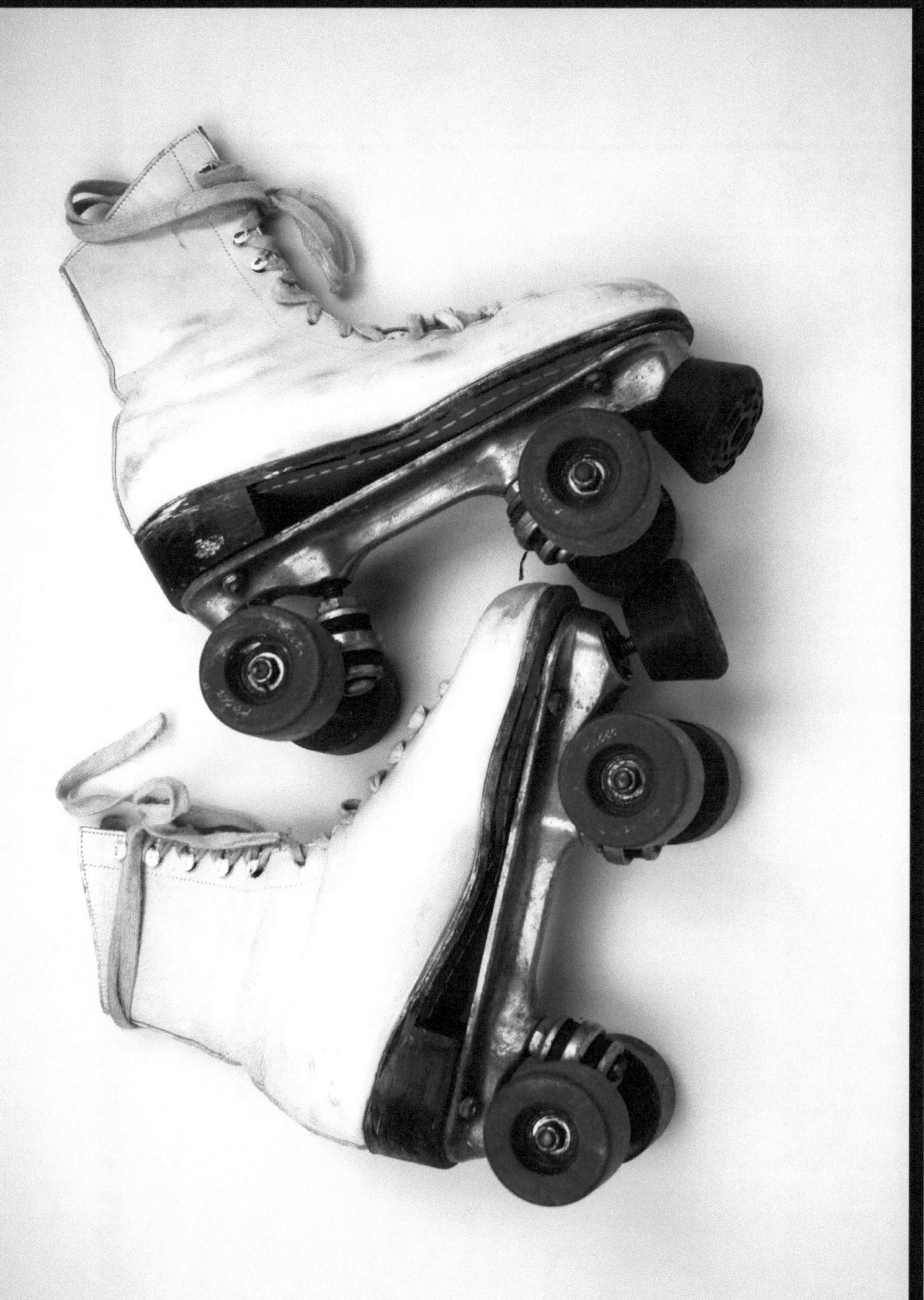

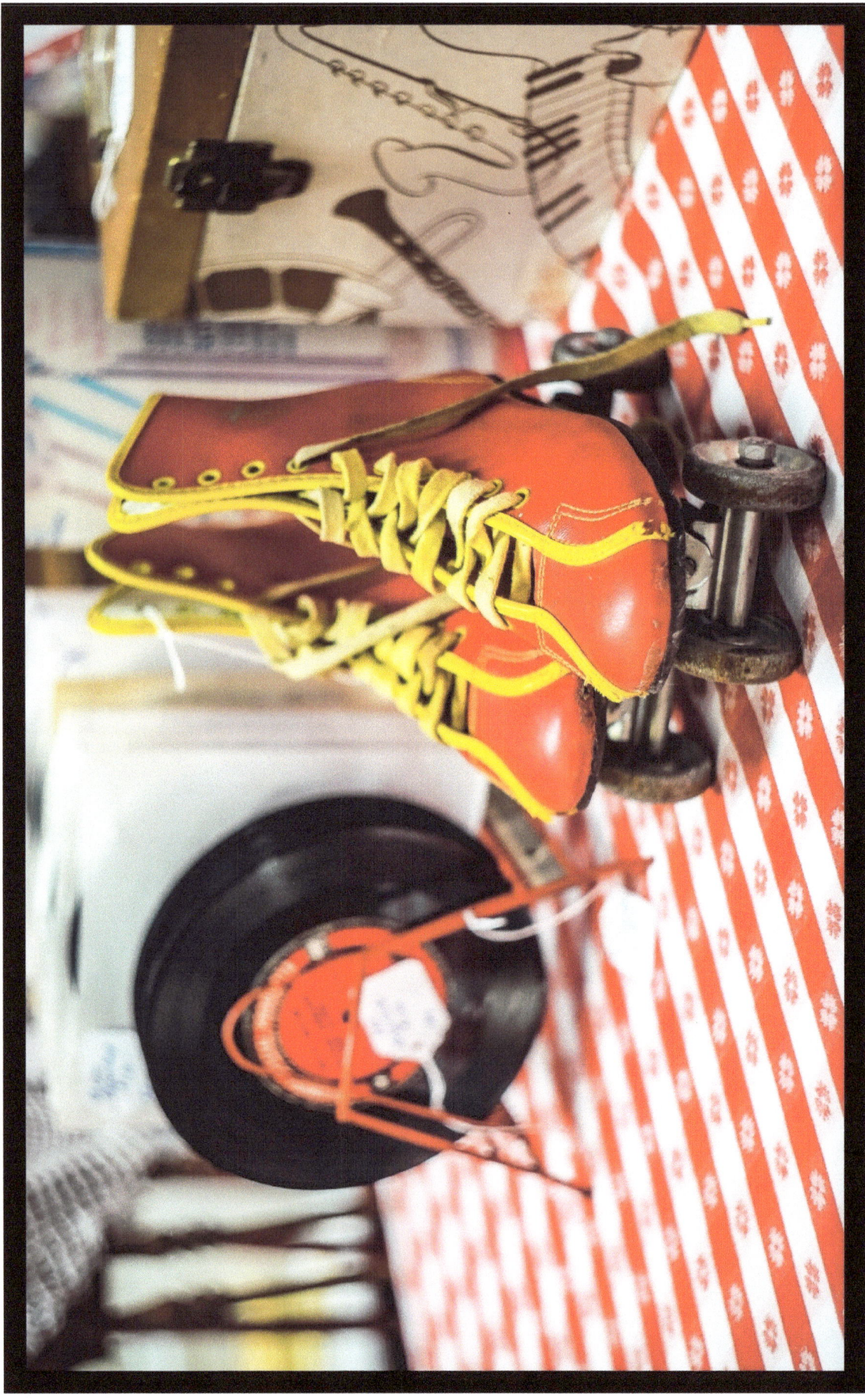

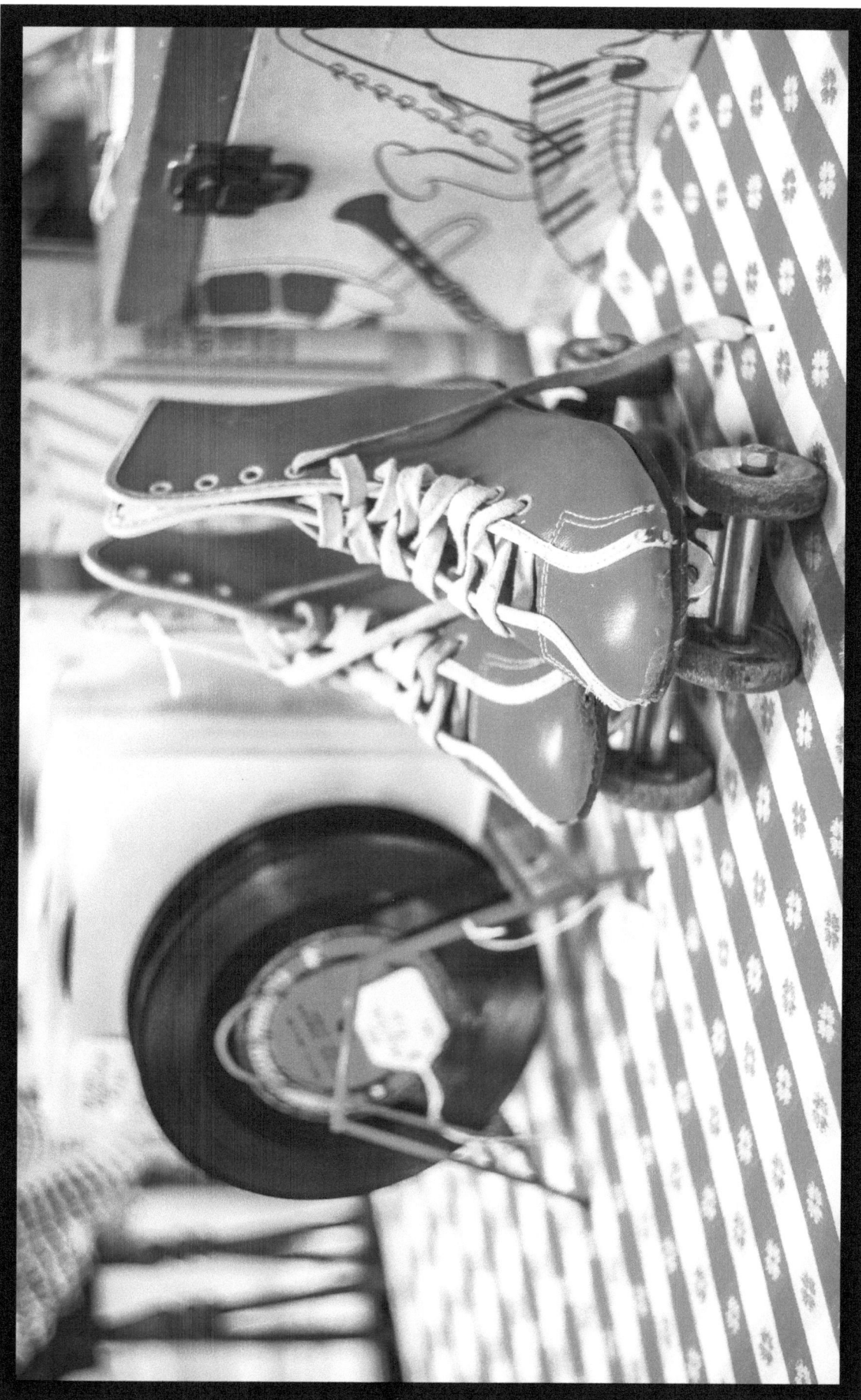

Thank you for purchasing Roller Skate Girls.
If you liked this adult coloring book, please check out our
other adult coloring books as well. They are available for
Purchase on Amazon and Createspace.

Our website is www.kdartsdesign.com

www.ingramcontent.com/pod-product-compliance
Lightning Source LLC
Chambersburg PA
CBHW050806180526
45159CB00004B/1563